Jack McArdle sscc

Insights

THAT INSPIRED ME
AND MAY ALSO INSPIRE YOU

GW00585196

the columba press

First published in 2007 by
the columba press
55A Spruce Avenue, Stillorgan Industrial Park,
Blackrock, Co Dublin

Cover by Bill Bolger
Cover photo by Kevin McLaughlin
Origination by The Columba Press
Printed in Ireland by ColourBooks Ltd, Dublin

ISBN 978 1 85607 583 1

Table of Contents

Dedication

My sincere thanks, warmest appreciation, and real love goes to my friends, the McLaughlin family, who left for work or school every morning at 8.00 am, and provided me with a house that was quiet, comfortable, and well provided – an ideal place in which to write a book. Without their kindness and hospitality, I doubt if this book would ever have been written.

Thank you, Brian, Carol Ann, Shane, Kevin, and Fiona.

Introduction

To be honest, I wrote this book because I wanted to clarify many things for myself. Another reason for writing was that friends requested that I do so. We are all familiar with the saying, 'A life without reflection is a life not worth living.' When we reflect, we are given *insights*. There are so many ways of looking at things, so many ways of understanding, so many levels of association. The one thing that has greatly motivated me over the years, in my writing, and retreats, was a conviction that the message was really very simple. It is a simple message for complicated people. I gave a talk recently to a group and, at the end of my talk, a man of seventy-four years of age turned to his daughter and said, 'It's really very simple, isn't it? I hope that we remember that.' The remark was relayed to me, and it was the highlight of my night, because I knew the man quite well, and I was thrilled that he captured the core message of what I was trying to get across. These insights are nothing more than that. I do not claim any 'insider' information on God, or things of God. I present these because they genuinely did help me, and I offer them to you in the hope that they help you also.

As it happens, chapters 8 to 14 are the seven themes that comprise the Life in the Spirit Seminars. I did not set out with this in mind, but I don't believe it is by accident that they should follow in such sequence. Some people might find these useful as a sort of do-it-yourself kit that leads to a greater openness to the Spirit. This could and should appeal to all colours and shades of Christian believers, because there is nothing couched in Charismatic language, and ideas and suggestions are deliberately kept simple and straightforward.

An insight is but a doorway that leads into a much vaster space. It is through reflection on the insight that I can personalise it, and it begins to speak directly to me. This, of course, is the Spirit at work, doing what he does best, i.e. 'telling you all about me, and reminding you of all I said to you', to quote Jesus. In his recent publication, our Holy Father brings us back to one simple truth: Jesus is the Son of God. He is not just a messenger from God, someone who came to tell us about God, or to call us back to God. When we see Jesus, we see God, and when we hear Jesus, we hear God speaking to us. An insight that helps bring me into a more personal relationship with Jesus, and helps deepen my awareness of the centrality of his message, is, indeed, a very special grace. These insights have been special graces for me, for which I will be eternally grateful. I express my gratitude to God by a strong desire to share these with others, in the hope that they, too, might experience some of the joy. I am grateful, gentle reader, for the privilege of sharing these riches with you. Let us pray for one another on our journey home to the Garden.

Come as you are

Coming before God in prayer is so much easier, once I recognise the *reality* of the situation. In other words, I am fully aware of how things actually are, and I have no desire to be anything or anybody other than who I am. God knows me through and through, and there's not much point in trying to impress, deceive, deny, excuse, or blame. I am an open book before him, just as I certainly will be at the moment of death. Instead of waiting till I die, I can stand before God any moment of any day, open the canvas of my life out to the very edges, and fully accept that he sees what's really there. This openness and honesty before God is at the heart of my relationship with him.

All I'm doing is trying to respond to God. The initiative is his, and I am not speaking about turning that into human endeavour. The fact is that God presents himself to me totally, completely, and unconditionally, no matter how little of that reality can be understood by my very limited human intelligence. God presents himself to me, irrespective of whether I bother with him or not. Nothing can change his attitude of total love towards me. Like a bird with a broken wing, he wants me to come to him, and let him love me.

Jesus is the Son of God is the central theme of a recent book of Pope Benedict XVI. In other words, when you watch Jesus among the sick, the sinners, and the outcasts in the gospel, you are watching God in action. Jesus is not just some sort of messenger from God; some sort of Holy Man who will tell us what he knows about God. When Jesus knelt before his apostles, with a basin of water and a towel, that was God in action. It was God who wept over Jerusalem because the people did not respond to his message. When I come before God, I must bring my leprosy, my sins, my demons, and all my human weaknesses with me. Otherwise I do not meet him. I only meet a god of my own creation, who doesn't really love, who doesn't really care, who

9

is not really interested. If I want to meet the *real* God, then I have to become *real* before him. The person or persons who invented this laptop I'm now using, knows it in great detail. However, not one of them could claim to know it thoroughly, as it evolves, develops, and modernises with each day. The advantage God has is that he continues to be in control of our creation, which is an on-going process. Nothing happens in us, or to us, without his knowledge. I cannot tell him anything about myself that he doesn't know, but he wants to be told, because he cares, and one way of showing that is the way he is prepared to listen.

If I think of God in terms of the Trinity, I can pray the following three short prayers: 'Father, for anything in me that you see is in need of your forgiveness, Lord have mercy. Lord Jesus, for anything in me that you see, in mind, heart, soul, memory, or body, that is in need of your healing touch, Christ have mercy. Spirit, Breath, and Power of God, for any brokenness, powerlessness, or helplessness that you see in me in need of your anointing and empowering, Lord have mercy.' I personally begin each Mass with these prayers, but you can use them whenever you feel like it.

Prayer becomes so much simpler when I come before God without any agenda. I offer him the key of willingness, giving him full access to my mind, heart, and soul. I *want* him to see what he sees. I can be tired, angry, discouraged, worried, and that is exactly how I come before him. Making *all* of myself present to him helps open me to receive *all* of what he offers me. We are speaking of *pure free gift* here. God does not check on our collection of Brownie points, Green Shield stamps, merits, or indulgences, before he decides whether to be present to us or not. There would be many a parent in jail for murder if they reacted wrongly to a child who comes in from playing, with mud and dirt all over their hands and clothes! Thank God my parents loved me enough, or I wouldn't be writing these words right now! When I come before God, I am not going on an inspection parade, with my shoes and buttons shining. The Prodigal Son didn't come over the horizon that way! The joy in the father's heart was not effected by his human condition, or the rags he was wearing. As a matter of fact, according to the story, the father immediately ordered a banquet and a whole new outfit of clothes. That was his way of responding to a very beloved son who was hungry, and poorly dressed.

'Come as you are' is the name of a hymn. To get this right, we have to focus on God when we come to him, and not on ourselves. It would be quite a risky business if my encounter with God was depending on my worthiness, or on my collection of virtues. Jesus had serious problems with the Pharisees in this whole area. However, as we say, there are none so blind as those who refuse to see.

What does God see when he looks at us? Let me attempt to answer that question this way. I presided at a funeral recently. The deceased was an elderly lady, held in great respect, and much loved by her family and friends. There was one phrase that I must have heard dozens and dozens of times at her funeral. 'She always saw the best in everyone.' What a wonderful tribute to the deceased! Speaking about her in this way was to say that she was a good person, and this was how her goodness expressed itself. Let's go back to that question: What does God see when he looks at us? If we accept that God is good, then we simply have to accept that he always sees the best in everybody. At each stage of creation, God 'saw what he had done, and he said "It is good".' 'God don't make no junk' (Herb Barks).

Standing before God just as I am, without fear or doubt, is to accept his love, and that is why Van Breeman defines faith as 'Having the courage to accept the acceptance of God' (*As Bread That Is Broken*). Do I have the courage to accept that God accepts what he sees when he looks at me? This is not to say I am perfect, or that I am all that God created me to be. Most likely, it is far from that. When Adam and Eve sinned, they hid. They thought they could hide from God. If they had presented themselves before God exactly as they were, at that moment, God would have accepted them, and would have given them the grace of *salvation*, which is the grace to start again. It is one of his greatest gifts. However, Adam blamed Eve, and Eve blamed the devil, and, to some extent, we're doing that since, and there is nothing God can do for us while we continue to behave in this way. Salvation is a very important gift of God. It is like an on-going expression of forgiveness. It is 'seventy times seven', multiplied by infinity. It may seem strange to say it, but it can be quite difficult for us to allow God be God. When I allow him the freedom of setting no limits to his love and acceptance, then I can be really bothered by the limitations I put on my response to him. The only limitations to what God can do for us are the ones we set. 'There is nothing impossible to God.'

I said earlier that, at the moment of death, I will come before God exactly as I am at that time. No more hiding, no more running, no more excusing, blaming, or trying to justify. The greatest preparation I could make for that moment is to begin now, and practise standing before God, opening out the canvas of my life, and inviting him to see every single thing that's there. 'This is me, Lord, warts and all.' When the lepers came to Jesus they had no way of denying, or of hiding the reality of their situation. The blind did not pretend they could see, nor did the lame pretend they could walk. Jesus could do something with them. On the other hand, the Pharisees presented themselves as beautiful marble sepulchres, not realising that Jesus could see the rotten and decaying bodies and bones within. They considered themselves as having a monopoly on truth and righteousness, and there is no way that Jesus could get them to see reality, because there was no way they were prepared to even consider it. 'The truth will set you free.' Never was truth spoken with such clarity and simplicity. The day came when each and every one of them had to come before God, and 'All that was hidden was brought out into the light of day.' That day will come for each and all of us.

The great advantage we have is that it can *begin right here, right now*. What a wonderful way to come before the Lord in prayer! And what a wonderful way to prepare for that Great Day when 'I will see the face of God and live.' It may sound simplistic, but it really helps to be as relaxed, as real, and as authentic as I can when I come to pray. I don't need a pious face or screwed up eyes. I can consciously relax every bone in my body, every emotion in my heart, and every thought and distraction in my mind. I don't have to be anything or anybody other than who I am right there. I'm sure each of us has one or two friends with whom we can be completely at ease, and feel completely at home. Surely such company is always enjoyable. God wants to be your *number one* friend.

What do you see?

The word 'Mystic' is defined as 'One who seeks by contemplation and self-surrender to obtain union with, or absorption into the Deity, or who believes in spiritual apprehension of truths beyond the understanding.' Among many others, St Padre Pio and St Teresa of Avila are our best known mystics. A mystic is someone who stares relentlessly at reality, and comes to see what is *really* there. As an ordinary human being, I am 'boxed in' by my humanity, and the limitations of my physical abilities. I can see what is there before my eyes, and I can hear what is within my hearing reach (with or without my hearing aids!). There are people in those houses across the road, but I cannot see them. There are people speaking to each other down at the end of the road, but I cannot hear them. I can hear cars in the distance, but I cannot see them. Like St Paul, 'I am a prisoner in this body', and my body determines the extent of my bodily senses.

The mystic is not imprisoned within such boundaries. The mystic sees what's *really* there, whether you or I can see that or not. The soul does not take up space, as the body does. Therefore, when someone dies, the body is left behind (which took up space), and the spirit (which does not require space) moves on to a *state* of being, whether that be heaven, hell, or purgatory. The deceased person goes *ahead*, but does not go *away*.

We are surrounded by spirits on every side. Padre Pio, from a very early age, always saw his Guardian Angel, but he never told anybody, because he thought everybody else did! I am now an incarnate, which means that I live in a body. The body is not *me*; I'm only living in it for a certain length of time. There will come a time when the fabric and functions of the body will begin to break down, and it will be no longer habitable. It is then I will have to vacate the body, change residence, and go to live elsewhere. The barriers and walls of the body will be broken, and I will be set free from this cage.

Try to visualise the following scene. A young lad is placed standing in a box which is so much higher than he is, and he is given a set of ear muffs which blocks out all sound. The box is placed in the middle of a large room, and the lad cannot see or hear a thing. The room is beautifully decorated, with very expensive drapes, furniture and chandeliers. The room is filled with people of all ages, races, and dress code. Suddenly the magician clicks his fingers, and the sides of the box fall away. Watch the look of amazement on the face of the young lad as he looks around the room. He had no idea of all the wonders and people that surrounded him. We are laughing, because *we* knew all the time what that room was like. That's what it'll be like at the moment of death. As the eyes of the body close, so the eyes of the soul open to endless vision, to clearly see all that was there all the time, but which was beyond the power of human vision. Part of that new 'seeing' will be that I will see myself clearly in relation to God, to others, and to life.

There is a 'mini-mystic' within each of us, and it is important that we develop that 'sense' of the Other. Just because I cannot see something doesn't mean that it's not there. The physically blind have a very heightened level of 'seeing', because they have to develop other sensitivities to make up for what the eyes cannot see. Their sense of touch, and of hearing, becomes very acute and, even without the white cane, they could probably sense that there is an object in their path.

I learned to pray by praying, and I learned to walk by walking. I can learn to sit in the company of the Others by doing so from time to time. I can do this at any hour of the day or night. I can do so sitting in my car, in a chair in my bedroom, or sitting on a rock overlooking the sea. I can bring my Companions with me, wherever I go. I should never feel alone, because I am *never* alone. Some people naturally enjoy their own company, and others require people around them at all times.

What I am suggesting now can become a real life-giving experience. In the first chapter, I suggested that we should not wait till we die to openly stand in the presence of God. The same thing applies to this present suggestion. If I hope to spend my eternity with Them, I should become familiar with their company. There is nothing I will get when I die that I'm not offered now. The only difference then is that I will see clearly, and comprehend a bit better. Even in heaven, I don't expect to be able to understand God, or have a full comprehension of his infinity. However, I will join all the choirs, human and angelic, in adoring and praising him for all eternity, with a sense of wonder and gratitude that will require an eternity to express.

Nowhere can we be more certain of the heavenly hosts being around us, than when we gather around the table of the Lord to celebrate Eucharist. Jesus tells us that where two or three of us are gathered in his name, he is there in the midst of us. If Jesus is present, then, you can be certain that *all* of heaven is there as well. When Jesus speaks of him making his home within us, he says that '*we*', the Father, Son, and Spirit will make their home in us.

I spent a week with a community of Cistercian monks for their annual Retreat at the end of last year. A few days before the Retreat began, two of the monks were called home suddenly by the Lord. Naturally, the rest of the community was deeply effected by this (and not just because they believe that they die in 'threes'!). During my time with them, I thought long and hard about the lesson to be learned from their sudden passing. One of the strongest awarenesses I had was how they must look back now, and see clearly just what an extraordinary occasion it was to stand at the altar for Eucharist. I felt certain that they looked back in awe at what really happened on such occasions, or how the whole of heaven was in attendance. I mentioned earlier about practising this inner disposition, and becoming more and more open to all the possibilities. Nowhere should this be easier than during the celebration of Eucharist. I should think long and hard before I enter the church door, and I should have my antennae fully stretched during the time I'm there.

It can help concentrate the mind if I remember that *all* my deceased relatives and friends are present, whether already in heaven, or being purified prior to entry into the Beatific Vision. I can be sure that they are very conscious of my presence. What a shame that I should ignore them, or fail to be aware of them. 'The Communion of Saints' is the bond that exists within Christ's Body, the church. There is the church triumphant (heaven), the church suffering (purgatory), and the church militant (on earth). When I am present at Eucharist, I am there as part of that church. Sometimes, today, we hear people bemoaning the fact that we have 'empty churches'. I don't think so!

It is important that we think and know of this as a *reality*, not as some sort of fantasy. We all have memories of playing 'Blind man's buff' as kids. For someone who is looking on, it can be hilarious. One of the people sits absolutely still, and the person with the blindfold is reaching in all directions, and is often within inches of the person's face before turning to search in another direction. So near and yet so far!

One time, when I was in hospital, I was having a completely sleepless night. I was twisting and turning, and there was no sense of drowsiness, and there was no hope of sleep. All chairs had been moved out on the corridor, as is usual at night. There was no sign of a nurse, so I sneaked out, grabbed a chair, placed it by my bed, and I asked Mary my Mother to sit on it and lull me to sleep! I was totally conscious of her being there, as I relaxed more and more … and I remember no more! It's as simple as that.

'Happy are they who have not seen and yet believe.' 'Reach out and touch the Lord as he goes by.' We are surrounded on every side by the church triumphant and the church suffering. It is called 'The Communion of Saints'. There is a certain order in this journey of discovery. If I could see them, there would be no thanks to me, and there wouldn't be much merit in my belief. If, on the other hand, I accept and believe, I will become more and more conscious of their presence, and this will become so real that it will be the same as if I could actually see with my eyes. There are other ways of seeing besides eyesight, and the eyes of the soul can see deeper, and much more distinctly.

It is not possible to exaggerate the richness that comes from being aware of living in such company. There is never an empty or lonely moment in my day or night, and I have a constant sense of joy from living in the presence of heaven.

Please remember that we are speaking of real living beings here. Living beings who can see us, who know us, and who really care for us. Apart from the Trinity, Mary, and the choirs of heaven, I am surrounded by relatives, friends, and former neighbours. The souls in purgatory should receive my special attention. When it comes to praying for the departed in the Mass, I digress a little, raise up the paten and chalice, and pray this prayer: 'Heavenly Father, we offer you these gifts on behalf of the souls in purgatory. We ask you to pour out upon them now the fullness of forgiveness, redemption, and salvation merited for them by Jesus on Calvary, so that many of them may *now* come into the kingdom of heaven.' I happen to believe that, through that prayer, there are souls in heaven at the end of the Mass that were not there when Mass began. What a privilege is ours!

As time goes on in this process, I can identify more and more of those who surround me. When someone belonging to us dies, we feel we have lost them, and it takes a while to find them again. Don't forget your favourite saints. What a privilege to be able to spend time with Thérèse of Lisieux, Faustina, Padre Pio, or John XXIII. You'll be absolutely amazed to discover that, in no time at all, you're sitting in the company of one of these, and listening to them speak about The Little Way, The Divine Mercy, the Power of Eucharist, or Renewal in the Church. Your creative imagination comes into play, and you become like the little girl who spends hours playing with 'her friends'. It is an extraordinary privilege to be able to make friends with all those with whom I will spend an eternity.

Hurry up, and catch up with those who have gone ahead of you (and, by that, I don't mean that you should die!). Nothing can separate God's children from each other, because they are closely bound in the embrace of his love.

Showing up

Jesus came to do what he had to do and, when that was finished, he returned to the Father. When he returned to the Father's side, he took his body with him, before sending his Spirit to complete his work on earth. It is important to remember that, a Spirit on its own cannot do anything. An evil spirit needs somebody's hands to plant the bomb, or somebody's tongue to tell the lie. It is the same with the Holy Spirit. Jesus sends the Spirit, but we must provide a body, through which that Spirit can work and act. I provide the body, and God provides the Spirit.

When I go to visit the sick in hospital, I do not go to heal anyone, because only God can heal. I go to provide the hands, which I lay on the head of the sick, and I totally depend on the Spirit to do whatever God wants to happen. It is not my responsibility whether the sick one is healed or not, nor is to my credit if the person is healed. I provide the tongue to speak God's word, the ears and heart to listen to that word, the feet to bring me to where the Spirit wants me to go and, if necessary, the hands to be used as channels of the healing power of the Spirit. As I sit here at the computer I am conscious of providing the hands on the keyboard, and I trust the Spirit to give power and inspiration to what I write. My most important contribution is to provide the key of willingness, so that the Spirit can have free access to my heart, soul, mind, and body. The Spirit cannot, or will not enter if he is not invited. The handle on the door of my heart is on the inside, and not even God can enter unless I open that door.

Remember that these chapters are about insights that have helped me, and continue to inspire me. This particular one under review now has been among the most helpful of all. It has enabled me to go to give talks when I hadn't an idea between my ears! It has enabled me walk into homes where chaos reigned supreme, and to say 'yes' to situations and undertakings that were very obviously completely beyond any natural gifts or talents I may possess. It has taught me that, if I want to walk on water, I have to step out of the boat! Exercising this insight has brought about a very real growth in the depth and reality of my faith. My favourite prayer, which has become my constant mantra, is 'Spirit and Breath and Power of God.' I just repeat this prayer, without asking for anything, and I have found that it keeps my heart tuned to the presence of the Spirit within.

There is one word of caution that I must mention here. When I speak of walking into awkward or impossible situations, or taking on work that is beyond my natural talents, there must be one vital condition present: I was *called on* to enter the situation, or I was *invited* to take on the work. It would be foolhardy and dangerous for fools to walk in where angels fear to tread. I am thinking here of agreeing to give a Retreat to a community of enclosed monks, being only too well aware that I, of myself, had nothing to offer them. The secret was that the Abbot asked me! I have had to ring on door bells to tell parents of a son's suicide, because I had found the son. When God puts me into a situation, he provides all that I need to handle that situation.

I had a weekend Retreat recently, and the theme of the Retreat was 'Just show up'! In other words, bring the body along, provide that key of willingness, and let the Spirit do everything else. I invite people to a genuine experience, and I am always encouraged by the witness of that experience. This is a transforming process. Once I hand over to the Spirit, I can expect good things to happen, and, as I continue with this mentality, my whole life becomes transformed. The only way I know to help an alcoholic is to persuade him to attend meetings. 'Keep bringing the body, and the rest of you will follow. Keep going to meetings, and don't stop till the miracle happens.' It is like pushing a car along a road, or learning how to use the ignition key! 'The Kingdom, the Power, and the Glory are yours.' If I provide any of the power, I will surely be tempted to steal some of the glory!

To 'show up' has to be a deliberate choice and decision, and not just drifting into a situation, like going to Mass just because it happens to be a Sunday morning. This is where the key of willingness becomes all important. I am the only one who has control of that key, and not even God will try to manipulate me into using it. In a way, I suppose, it is just as important *how* you come to prayer, as what happens when you pray. To have the right disposition, to have the proper priority, to remember what really matters … all of that is part of my prayer life.

I mentioned earlier about stepping out of the boat, if I want to walk on water. I was a swimming instructor at an earlier stage in my life. One of my memories is of a twelve-year lad, with a look of determination on his face, letting go of the bar and swimming to the other side of the pool for the first time. His joy was unbounded. He couldn't wait to get home to tell his parents. If we had mobile phones in those days, he would be 'on' in seconds! I applauded him, which enhanced the thrill of his excitement. I didn't tell him that a friend of mine had two young children, and she had them swimming around in the deep end of a swimming when they were a few weeks old! A newborn baby does not need to be taught how to swim. Water has been its natural environment for some time now, and there is no fear involved in the process of introducing the baby to water from a very early age. If, on the other hand, the baby is not exposed to this early experience, it may be twelve years later before he's prepared to take the risk.

I can follow my homily notes with attention to detail, and I can cling to the prayers and directions of the official ritual for dear life; but the whole thing lacks spontaneity and personal conviction if I'm not prepared to lift my head off the page from time to time, and say what's in my heart. When I speak *from* the heart, I speak *to* the heart. If speaking the Lord's word is part of my Christian apostolate, then I have to come, more and more, to depend on the Spirit to give me the words, and to inspire those words. 'When you speak on my behalf,' says Jesus, 'don't worry what you shall say, because the Spirit will give you words that no one can resist.'

I could say in one sentence what I hope to say in this chapter! Christy Moore sings 'Don't forget your shovel if you want to go to work.' What I am saying is what Jesus told the apostles before he left them on the Mount of Olives: 'Stay in Jerusalem, and don't leave till the Spirit comes.' Is it possible that Catholics get off the train too early? They set out with Jesus at Christmas, travel on to Lent, Holy Week, Good Friday, and Easter Sunday. Then they get off the train, waving banners, and proclaiming that 'He has risen! Alleluia!' The problem is that the terminus is Pentecost, and they got off the train too soon. Apart from Jesus, nothing happened to anybody else on Easter morn. The apostles would have denied, sold, or deserted him all over again that very evening, if the pressure was on them. They were to do nothing until the Spirit came. It is only then, when they received the 'power from on high', that they could become Jesus' witnesses to the ends of the earth.

Notice the two parts of the promise. 'You will receive power from on high, and you shall be my witnesses.' With the privilege comes the responsibility to make use of that privilege. I have neither right nor authority of any kind to represent Jesus in any way until I have received that 'power from on high'. I can be a channel, but never a generator. Show up by all means, provide the voice, the ears, the heart, or the hands. Once you do that willingly, you have to get out of the way, and allow the Spirit take over, and effect whatever good the Lord has in mind. It is an extraordinary privilege to have a close-up view of the Spirit at work. 'You will see signs and wonders ...'

Showing up, or providing the body, is a very practical and real way of saying 'yes', which is a core prayer when we deal with the Spirit. 'Be it done onto me according to your word.' Only God can do a God-thing, and what is done, and what I allow to happen, is the work of the Spirit in me. The only limits to what the Spirit can do in us, through us, or for us, are the limits we set. It must surely give us food for thought to think that any one of us can set limits to the work of the Spirit in our lives. That is very sad indeed and, when we become aware of it, it certainly should make us sad. I don't believe that the average person would *want* to do that, but is doing so unconsciously. Any sense of gratitude I have for all of God's goodness should open my heart more and more to his love and blessings. I can never be 'full' of the Spirit until he has removed more and more of the self, the ego, that takes up so much space within. When the Spirit is given free rein in my spirit, the space available to him is constantly expanding. I will stop here, because I want to develop this insight at greater length in the following chapter.

The Skips

It's very difficult to put into words what the Holy Spirit does in us, or how he works. However, I think it is important that we have some images of his action, and so I am going to attempt to put words on something that is both miraculous and mysterious.

The Spirit works from within. Jesus speaks of the Spirit as a fountain of living water that rises up from within a person. In other words, it does not begin in the head, in the understanding. Reading books, discussions, attending lectures, etc, does not bring us any closer to the Spirit. All of the above just informs the head, but it doesn't form the heart. There are two levels of knowledge, i.e. academic knowledge and experiential knowledge. I get the academic knowledge from books, but I glean the experiential knowledge through experience. The important point I am making here is that the Spirit has to be experienced firstly, and, perhaps, understood some other time.

I say 'perhaps', because I don't expect to understand God, not even in heaven. To understand something is to have a grasp of all that it contains, from end to end; to grasp how it functions, and to require no further explanation. I suggest that we could never do that with God! Thomas Aquinas tells us that, when we speak about God, we can be sure of only one thing ... that we're wrong! No matter what we say/think about God, he is much much more than that. I am like a tiny fish in the middle of the Atlantic ocean, making new discoveries of the same sea every day. It would be a foolish little fish, and a very dead little fish, if it tried to rise so far above the water so as to get a glimpse of the sea from Galway to New York! My first point, then, is that, while speaking of the work of the Spirit, I am attempting to provide some understanding of that work, while standing powerless before the Mystery.

I headed this chapter 'The Skips'. This represents one of my understandings of the work of the Spirit. As I write, the house in which I live is undergoing major renovation. Because I have lived with the old, the cold, and the mould for so long, the happiest sight for me is to see skip after skip being filled up with old bricks, carpets, baths, and loads of dismembered pieces of furniture. I feel like shouting 'Right On!' every time I pass the skip! There is so much dumping to be done before the work of reconstruction can begin. I cannot think of the Spirit working within me without being aware of the constant need for the skip!

Imagine the inner self as being a deep deep well, with a gurgling spring of living water at the base. The problem is that the well is filled with the wreckage and the garbage of life, and the water cannot get near the surface. The Greek word for conversion is *kinosis*, which literally means 'to empty out'. This is where the skip comes in handy!

I have vivid memories of the first time I came across an oasis. I was travelling to a place in the United Arab Emirates to give a parish mission. This meant four or five hours of driving along an undulating desert road. Apart from a few camels, and a few nomads, there was little sign of life. All of a sudden I came over the brow of a hill, and was confronted with an apparition (I thought of the word 'mirage', but no, this was real!). It was an oasis that spread as far as the eye could see. Green, green, green everywhere. The noise was extraordinary. Children playing, animals roaring, engines purring and puffing. The trees and the water were alive with birds of all kinds and colours. Fruits of every kind hung from the trees. Some people seemed to be busy, while others just dozed in the shade of a tree. This surely called for a break, a coffee, some fruit, and a few souvenirs. The people were friendly, and willing to sell me anything they had! As I took to the desert road again, there was one thought that was uppermost in my mind: Beneath every square inch of desert I had driven in the past few hours was the same amount of water. The problem is the water couldn't reach the surface. In this place it had got to the surface, and became a source of life for man and beast alike. As I drove along, my thoughts continued to dwell on all that water, on how it was blocked from surfacing, and what it would take to facilitate another oasis.

I have gone on for some time about this, because it very accurately reflects aspects of the human condition. I meet the occasional person who is a real life-giving oasis, and I meet others and there's nothing but sand. When I think of that gurgling spring of living water at the core of each human being, I have to reflect how best that can be released. Jesus speaks of the Spirit as 'a fountain of living water that wells up within a person'. The only answer I can come up with is to continue to say 'yes' to the skip! That 'yes' must become a burning desire, a very real longing, a palpable thirst. When Jesus met the Samaritan woman at the well, he had a problem getting her to understand what kind of water he was offering her. Referring to the well he said 'Whoever drinks of this water will be thirsty again. But whoever drinks of the water that I shall give will never be thirsty; for the water that I shall give will become in him a spring of water welling up to eternal life.'

In reading the account of Pentecost in the Acts of the Apostles, I remember being puzzled by one particular thing. On Pentecost morning, we are told that 'They were all filled with the Holy Spirit.' Two chapters later, when Peter and John were released from prison, they met with the disciples, who prayed with them, and, wait for it, 'They were all filled with the Holy Spirit.' I wondered what happened the Holy Spirit they had received a few days ago! I *think* I understand it better now. The Spirit can only fill what space is available to him. We speak of someone 'being full of himself', meaning that this person is very much at the centre of his own being, of his concerns, and of his own sense of importance. The more that 'self' shrinks, and gets out of the way, the more space there is for the Spirit to fill. As the Spirit continues to transform us from within, the wreckage and garbage of the past begins to be disposed of and, in theory, at least, like Mary, I could become 'full of grace'. Carl Houselander calls Mary the Reed of God. The pan pipes are reeds that are totally empty, and, with the holes along the reeds, it is possible to make sounds of rare beauty with them. She also speaks of Mary as a chalice, or a bird's nest, both of which are empty, and receptive to something being placed in them. Both images depict the opposite of 'being full of oneself'.

One image that stays in my mind, when I think of the Spirit working away within me, is the image of barnacles clinging to the side of a boat, or of a rock. It is really difficult to remove them, as if they were glued on. My prayer with such an image is 'Right on, Lord! Go ahead, Lord! Get rid of everything that clings to me that is not of you.' Some people are hoarders by nature. If they throw something in the skip today, they'll probably go out and retrieve it tomorrow! Personally, I just love getting rid of rubbish. Once or twice a year I clear the wardrobe of clothes I have no intention of wearing, and the shelves of books I have read, or have no intention of reading. It's a wonderful feeling. I head straight down to the Simon Community shop with the clothes, before I do a rethink and start retrieving a sweater or two that I may need later! The books are landed down in the library, lest they end back on my shelves. I believe this helps me relate much more readily to the idea of the Holy Spirit and the skips. Skips play a pivotal role in my spiritual journey!

God's creation is on-going, as we continue to be made in his image and likeness. It is a life-long process, and it continues right up to the moment of death. 'Gestation' is a very good word to describe what is happening. We are in a state of continuous change 'until Christ is formed within us'. The Spirit does in us what he did in Mary.

There is one very real danger inherent in this whole process. I have referred to it already but, I believe, it could do with being repeated. The only limits to what the Spirit does in us are the ones we set. The Spirit cannot work outside of those limits. When Mary was told what God required of her, she asked how this could be done. She was told that the Holy Spirit would come upon her, and the power of the Most High would overshadow her, because 'There is nothing impossible with God.' Mary believed that promise, and so, God was free to do whatever he wished with her. She set no boundaries or no limits. What the Spirit did, in and through Mary, is what the Spirit would love to do in and through everyone of us. Unlike Mary, however, there is much wreckage and garbage to be removed, many many skips to be filled, before we come anywhere near being capable of being 'full of grace'.

I referred at the beginning of this chapter to the root and branch renovation going on in the house where I live (the house with the skips out front!). I don't have to tell you that I have nothing whatsoever to do with that work! I just step over the debris, or around the frame of the scaffolding, as I move around. I mention this because it is exactly the same with the work of the Spirit. I am not doing any of the work. Just as I fully approve, and would not deter the workmen in any way, so it is with the work of the Spirit. At the beginning of the work on the house, it was a case of demolition. Walls, doors, etc. were disappearing. After some time, the opposite process began. New walls were being built, new doors were hung, new wiring and plumbing replaced the old, the outdated, and the dangerous.

I find it very encouraging to discover new insights, fresh ways of looking at things of God, and aspects of the message becoming easier. This is an on-going process, and most of the time I am not aware of the gestation. I sometimes think that a mother who has conceived and borne a baby would have a much greater ability to understand the inner work of the Spirit. Each day she monitors the development of that inner life, and then the time comes when the unborn will let her know that it's there! What happened with Mary during her pregnancy, leading up to the birth of Jesus is a very powerful and real way of understanding the work of the Spirit in us. In Mary's case, however, there was no need for the skip, so conception could begin straight away.

The Gift

Those who know me, know me as a talker, as a weaver of words, a storyteller, and someone who never hesitates to stretch the imagination in attempts to grasp some simple basic truth. None of them would think of me as a singer! I don't sing because I don't have that gift, and I don't play the piano because music was not included in the good Lord's generous allocation of gifts to me. There are people who cannot see, because they do not have the gift of sight, and there are others who don't speak because they lack the gift of speech. This is a long-winded way of making a simple point: I cannot pray, if I don't have the gift of prayer.

Oh, of course, I can say prayers, and I can read prayers, but that's not the same as praying. I could possibly teach an intelligent parrot to say a prayer, but I could never teach a parrot to pray! I consider it a wonderful grace, and a marvellous discovery that, after many years of endeavour at the task of prayer, I suddenly discover that it was a gift all that time, and there was no need for all that foot-slogging that had my mind boggled with numbers, and my mouth full of words. There were times when my prayer was heavy-going, and quite exhausting. Many of us have memories of siblings falling off to sleep in the middle of the Rosary trimmings!

The organ God gave me with which to pray is my heart, not my tongue. I haven't been back to Assisi for a few years, and they had an earthquake there a few years ago. I don't know what changes this has brought about in the structure of the basilica, but I hope that one inscription has survived. Over the high altar were the words 'Si cor non orat, in vanum lingua laborat', which literally translates as 'If the heart is not praying, the tongue is labouring in vain' (or 'wasting its time', as we would normally express it).

Words are often the weakest form of communication. I can

stand by a grave, holding someone's hand, or with an arm around a shoulder, and words could become an insensitive intrusion. There could be powerful communication going on between a mother and a tiny baby, even if both are silent. The umbilical cord may be cut, but the bond is just as real. Motherhood is a truly beautiful gift for those who have the physical and mental health to give themselves to it. It must be something that goes with the territory, that comes with the baby, just like the mother's milk. Prayer is a gift that is given to the heart that has a hunger for God. It is not about performance, it is about free-sailing, just hoisting the sails, and being willing to go.

The apostles saw Jesus work great wonders. They saw him raise the dead, calm the storm, and cleanse the lepers. Yet they never asked him to teach them how to do those things. They watched him as he prayed, however, and that must have made such a deep impression on them that they asked 'Lord, teach us to pray.' Jesus' prayer seemed to have more to do with listening than with speaking. He was in the habit of 'spending the night in the prayer of God' before making any big decisions, like choosing his apostles, or preaching the Sermon on the Mount, for example.

Prayer is not me talking to God who won't hear, but God talking to me who won't listen. Real prayer is 'Speak, Lord, your servant is listening', and not 'Listen, Lord, your servant is speaking'. What a beautiful prayer in itself ... praying for the gift to be able to pray. There is a vast difference between praying and saying prayers. Saying prayers always require words, usually words written by someone else. Most of this comes from outside of me. The secret of prayer, of course, is that my spirit possesses all that is needed to pray. The Spirit of God lives within me, and it is the Spirit who transforms my words into prayer. Prayer is one of the most important gifts of the Spirit. The Spirit actually prays within us, and we can come to join our hearts to that action. This is pure gift, and it cannot be earned, learned, or acquired. 'Lord, teach us to pray' is the only school there is.

The first thing I require is a real desire to pray. This can de-

velop in many ways. The most usual way is probably an awareness of God's love and generosity, prompting a desire within me
to express my thanks and appreciation. It is as if I wanted to proclaim his goodness to me, and how I express that is of little sig-
nificance. I can have a deep sense of gratitude and, if I so choose,
I can use words to express it. There are times when I want to
shout out, when I want to proclaim God's goodness to the
world. At such times the words are unimportant, as we witness
when someone sings, dances, claps their hands, or sings out
words that have no apparent meaning. They are, as we describe
it, 'giving vent' to their feelings. There is a stream of prayer and
praise within the human heart, and when this breaks out, it can
emerge in many forms. In a way, I suppose, the gift of prayer, of
which I speak, is the result of an awakening to the reality of
what the good Lord is doing in my soul, and in my life. Like
Mary's Magnificat, I 'magnify' the Lord, and the bigger my God
the smaller my problems.

Several times recently, I have heard various versions of the
following story. A couple had a little three-year-old girl and a
newborn baby boy. The girl kept asking to be left alone with the
baby. Her parents were afraid to allow this, because they
thought perhaps she was jealous of her new brother, and might
harm him. With the best intentions in the world, she might pick
him up to nurse, and accidentally drop him. Finally, they agreed
to the child's request, but they listened in through the intercom
in the newborn's bedroom. The girl entered the room and, at
first, there was silence. Then the parents heard their daughter
whisper to the baby, 'Tell me about heaven, because I'm beginning to forget.'

Why does this story touch people so deeply, and why is it so
widespread? Perhaps it is because the story reminds us of something that we all once knew. The psychiatrist Joan Fitzherbert
writes that 'until the age of two, children are in intimate contact
with the mind of God. Their consciousness is only partly here –
and the rest is with the One from whom they came.' What is im-
plied here is that the Divine is always part of our deeper inner

selves, and that prayer is one of the ways in which that is expressed. My parents and teachers taught me many prayers, but it was many years later before I learned how to pray. This learning process was nothing more than a growing awareness of some sort of inner hunger in my spirit, and I felt nourished whenever I prayed. A very popular book of some years ago was Ralph Martin's *Prayer is a Hunger*.

When I speak of the gift of prayer, I am not just thinking of some fluidity in expressing my inner disposition towards God. It is so much more than that. The very desire to pray is an important part of this gift. Taking time out, and finding time for prayer is another part of the gift. Prayer involves making time and space for God, working on my relationship with God, spending conscious time in the presence of God. All of this is pure gift. 'Lord, teach us to pray' is the beginning of a process.

St Francis of Assisi tells us that we should always preach the gospel, and, only when we have to, we should use words. It is the same with prayer … only when we have to, we should use words. Using words might be nothing more than just that … using words. It is the Spirit who changes my words into prayer. If the Spirit is not in my words, then I'm only talking to myself! In the movie, *The Ruling Class*, Peter O'Toole is in a psychiatric hospital, and his problem is that he thinks he's God. To humour him, the psychiatrist asked him 'When did you first discover that you were God?' 'I was praying and praying for years and years, and then one day I woke up and discovered I was only talking to myself!'

To slightly misquote a saying that was fashionable some years ago 'A prayer without the Spirit ne'er to heaven will go'. I have a few reminders of that before me as I write. I have a mobile phone, with no wires. However, if there is not some system of connection and communication available to it, I can talk into it all day long, and nobody can hear me. It is the same with the e-mails on the computer. I can send a message to every addressee in my phone book, but no one gets the message unless there is some vehicle of conveyance which will deliver that message to

all those destinations. The Spirit provides many gifts, like wisdom, understanding, faith, etc. What I am stressing here is that one of the most important gifts of the Spirit is the gift of Prayer. It transforms my whole life, and leads to the discovery and exercising of many other gifts. Nowadays we have many workshops and courses on prayer and they all serve a purpose. The best school of all, of course, is the school of the Spirit. There are no failures, no bad grades, or no examinations there. Prayer is something that happens to me, when I attend that school.

I remember, many years ago, I was on my first summer course in French in the seaside town of San Malo in Brittany (France). I had a bad morning, was very discouraged, and felt like throwing in the towel and going home! I went for a stroll on the beach. Very soon I came across a young lad of about four who was having a major row with his dog. The dog was after doing something wrong, and the young lad was really letting him have it. The dog cowed in such a way that it was evident he understood that he was in trouble. That didn't help me at all! A four-year old and a dog could understand French and I couldn't make head or tail of it! I thought about it for a while, and realised that both child and boy never actually were taught French, nor were they ever conscious of learning it. They were just in the right environment, and the process just unfolded. I returned to class and life began to improve!

The school of the Spirit provides the perfect environment in which to grow in prayer. Notice I said 'grow in prayer' rather than 'learn to pray'. I have friends with whom I stay for a few days regularly. They have the gift of hospitality to a very high degree. There are three teenagers in the family, and music is in every fibre of their being … piano, guitar, drums, banjo, tin whistle, etc, etc. I could walk into that house today with a clarinet, and I'll bet that one of them will be playing a tune on it tomorrow. All of that is possible because each of them has the gift of music to a very high degree. I have learned something about prayer from them!

A pat on the back

It is interesting to note how religious beliefs change and evolve over the years. What I was taught as a child was something that was written in bronze, something that would always be true, something that would never change. However, Revelation is an on-going process; it involves pulling back the veil a little bit more, and leading to fresh understandings and awareness. As we continue to evolve in a more and more materialistic world, the religious dimension appears to be watered down, and has become more relative. Twice in the past week I met two grandmothers who were really worried because their grandchildren had not been baptised. This is a problem that neither of them could have foreseen or expected. To a certain extent they still live with the values and customs of an earlier generation, and baptising a newborn baby was one of the central issues of rearing a family.

One of the grandmothers confessed to me that she had performed a provisional rite of baptism on the children, totally unknown to the parents, and she wanted my opinion on that! This led to a discussion about the early evolution of baptism in the church. She was surprised to discover that baptism was never intended for infants. It was for mature Christians, who had spent a few years of a catechumenate programme in preparation for the ceremony. It was a graduated programme of preparation, with scrutinies and interviews before a bishop, before the person was accepted as being ready for baptism. In those days, when the existence of Limbo was accepted as a reality, there was great fear that a child might die before reaching the required age for baptism, and, therefore, such a child would not make it into heaven. (This church teaching has been reviewed and discontinued only quite recently. It was first rejected in *The Catechism of the Catholic Church* some years ago, and it is only a few months since the Pope made a very public reference to that change).

Incidentally, this was seen as important, because it was a real stumbling block for Muslims, who believe that such innocent ones are transferred as angels into the highest heavens. Personally, I find that the church's ability and willingness to alter a stance on something that has been seriously reviewed is quite refreshing and consoling. Like all those people sent to hell years ago for eating meat on Fridays, or for going to Communion without having fasted since the previous midnight. When we remember that both these rules applied equally in countries where people were dying of hunger, this borders on the obscene and the grotesque. Not one word of the gospels has changed, but our understanding of moral issues, of spiritual life, or of church practice must always be open to review.

Like the grandmother I met recently, it became customary for parents to improvise a sort of do-it-yourself form of baptism, just in case the person died before reaching the age of admission to the sacrament. This developed, and became the norm, to such an extent that, when the bishop did eventually arrive on the scene, all he had to do was confirm what had already taken place. It was at this point that baptism became 'splintered', and ended up as two sacraments. In other words, what the bishop did became a separate sacrament and, instead of just confirming what had gone before, it came to be the sacrament of confirmation.

I believe we could benefit greatly by returning to the connection that always existed between both ceremonies. It would be one of the ways to justify infant baptisms, if an opportunity was afforded later, at a more mature age, for the person to make his/her own personal commitment. It is probably true to say that many people would be afraid to move away from infant baptism. Personally, I am still very much in favour of it, even though I am more than willing to consider the options or the alternatives.

Even though the baby is not involved in any of the process leading up to, and including baptism, I have discovered that it can be a wonderful time of renewal and recommitment for the parents and family. The more work that is done with the family, the better chance the baby has of growing up in a Christian environment. You don't renew people, or you don't corrupt people. You renew the atmosphere in which they live or you corrupt the atmosphere in which they work, and the rest follows.

My reason for trawling through the history and evolution of these sacraments was to isolate that word *confirmation*. It has a very important meaning, other than just being the name of a sacrament. John the Baptist told the people that he baptised with water, but there was One among them who would baptise with the Holy Spirit and with fire. The cleaning properties of water are quite limited. Even if the stain is removed, a forensic scientist could easily discover where the stain had been. Fire, on the other hand, changes things utterly. When a rusty gilder of steel is thrown into the furnace, it comes pouring out of the crucible with all rust and dross completely removed. Baptism with the Spirit sets the heart on fire, and a purifying process ensues. 'Enkindle within us the fire of your Divine Love.'

St Paul met a group of believers in Ephesus, and he asked them an unusual question. 'Did you receive the Holy Spirit when you became believers?' They answered 'We have not even heard that anyone may receive the Holy Spirit.' Paul then asked 'What kind of baptism have you received?' And they answered 'The baptism of John.' Paul then explained, 'John himself spoke of another one who was to come, and that one is Jesus.' Upon hearing this, they were baptised in the name of the Lord Jesus.

I spoke at the beginning of this paragraph of my desire to isolate the word 'confirmation'. I isolate it simply to give it a broader meaning, and a wider application. As well as being a sacrament, the word 'confirm' means to make another feel worthwhile and appreciated. Your willingness and your ability to confirm another person, and make that person feel worthwhile, is the surest sign that you have the Holy Spirit within you. If you don't have the Spirit within you, you certainly cannot give anybody confirmation. Most likely, you will avail of each and every opportunity to knock them, to put or pull them down. Every one of us can give confirmation to those around us. It is among the most important work of the Spirit.

I often joke that if you want to hear something good about a person in Ireland, you have to go to his funeral! Everybody is saying lovely things about him. It would be wonderful if you could have your funeral during your lifetime! You could take a tape-recorder to the funeral, and record all the lovely things they're saying about you, and, when you are down and depressed, you could take out the tape and play it. 'Send me the flowers now, be they pink, or blue, or red. I'd rather have one blossom now that a truckload when I'm dead.' Please send me the flowers when I can still smell them. They'll be no good to me on my coffin!

Confirming others is an anointed and special way of treating others. Any of us can do it, and everyone around us needs it. If we're honest, we will readily admit that we all love the words of affirmation and encouragement from time to time. In fact, I would go so far as to say that there is a hunger and thirst within us all for the word of praise and of recognition. 'Treat others as you would like them to treat you' is a very wise dictum indeed. There is a saying in Irish, 'Praise the young and they'll come.'

Only last night I spent some time listening to a young lad playing the guitar and singing. He had a good voice, and is an excellent musician, but he was nervous and slightly embarrassed. I spoke very positively about the quality of his singing voice, and about the definite talent that he possessed. As I continued to confirm him, his voice grew firmer and more confident. Soon he was in full swing, and I marvelled at the transformation that was taking place right before my eyes.

It is sad that we can so easily forget just how we can confirm and encourage others in their growth, and in their lives in general. Our own self-esteem, or lack of it, is the biggest barrier. If I cannot think positively about myself, I have nothing to pass on to you. The day I feel good about me, I think you're ok too! But God help you on those days when I'm not on the best of terms with myself! Even the dog could get a kick on such a day! 'What a wonderful world it would be' if each of us took seriously our capacity to build up those around us, and to make them feel worthwhile. There is absolutely no scarcity of material out there. Just as some people cannot give confirmation because of their negative approach to themselves, so some people cannot accept praise or affirmation, because of the same reason.

It is important, however, that we continue to give; but it is also important that we're not telling lies, or saying things that we ourselves don't believe. Surely we can find enough to speak about, without inventing falsehoods. There is a kind of circular effect going on here. The more positive and healthy our own self-image is, the more we see in the other that is worthy of confirmation. If we cannot see anything good in the other, the problem may very well lie within ourselves.

Repeating yourself

May I remind myself, and you, gentle reader, what I set out to do in this book? It is an attempt to take a close look at my own life, and discover what insights have helped me the most in my journey. I then offer those to you, in the hope that some of them may also help you.

The title of this chapter is 'Repeating yourself'. This has to do with a form of prayer that is of the mantra form, where a word or words are just repeated over and over again, until they sink into my subconscious, and become part of me. I have found this to be most helpful, when I got the 'hang' of it. The organ God gave me with which to pray is the *heart*, not the *tongue*. It is a question of having a praying heart, rather than a praying tongue. Jesus tells us that the Spirit is like a spring of living water, which wells up from within a person. In other words, it begins in the heart, and may find, and need expression with the tongue.

As someone who has suffered from heart failure for several years now, I appreciate the luxury of being able to breathe deeply. It can be quite distressing to try to be active, while gasping for air with short, shallow breaths. The thrill of filling the lungs right down to the base is a wonderful experience for those with breathing problems. Prayer of the heart is deep-down stuff. We are familiar with the expression of speaking under one's breath. It is a kind of deep-down whisper that is clearly audible.

I must confess to being a sports addict, when it comes to certain sports on the television. I often have to discipline myself, not to get too excited or involved! I tell myself 'They're getting well paid to play this game, and, if they can't win out there, there's very little I can do here to help them!' However, I must confess that, even at my calmest moments, I am whispering 'Come on! Come on! Come on!' That's as near as I can get to explaining what I experience as quiet whispering mantra prayer.

Come, Holy Spirit! Come Holy Spirit! Come, Holy Spirit! This quiet whisper can go on, almost on automatic pilot, even in the midst of my most active endeavours. I find it ideal for these waking moments during the night, when I'm in the car, or waiting for the kettle to boil! Prayer is about communicating with the heart. My own best image to represent this is a mother and young baby. The same words, coos, whispers are repeated again and again and, whether the baby understands or not, they seem to have a calming effect, until the crying stops and the baby settles. You couldn't imagine the mother making a speech to the baby: 'Vouchsafe, I beseech thee humbly, to grant onto me one night's sleep.' I don't think the baby would understand, and the crying might well continue.

I realise that I am using the word 'mantra' in a very broad and general sense. Rather than categorise it under 'Centring Prayer', 'Contemplative Prayer', etc, I am presenting it as just another way of praying. I can whisper the name 'Jesus' thousands of times. Nothing more than that. My own favourite prayer is 'Spirit and Breath, and Power of God'. Nothing more. I'm not asking for anything, or adding anything to those words. I find this prayer very uplifting. In fact, I would go so far as to call it a very peaceful accompanying prayer. I could not repeat this prayer and be lonely at the same time.

I cannot remember the circumstances when I first began using these words, nor was I ever very conscious of this prayer growing on me or, indeed, in me. It is only now, upon reflection, that I realise just how central this prayer has become. When I think of some up-coming talk, Retreat, etc, I just instinctively begin whispering this prayer. It serves to 'anchor' me, and keep my soul at peace. Maybe, without this prayer, I might possibly become anxious or preoccupied with what lies ahead. Singing a word or two to any tune that comes to my mind is another form of accompanying prayer that I find very helpful. I can repeat the words 'Praise you' to the tune of any song I choose. After a while, the words seem to melt away, and I'm not actually saying them, but they are being repeated somewhere within my being. I can have great ease and comfort with this kind of prayer, because there is absolutely no effort required.

My generation grew up with what one might call a 'Spirituality of Addition'. More and more prayers and novenas to more and more saints, and we could build our own Tower of Babel and arrive safely in heaven! (I do not wish to cynically dismiss this, because it produced many holy souls, such as our parents; but it was a tough road, involving a lot of hard work.) The kind of prayer of which I speak in this chapter would come under the heading of a 'Spirituality of Subtraction'. It is not that I discard the prayer books and novena leaflets, but I am willing to allow them decrease as I allow the influence of the Spirit to increase, as he leads me along the path of prayer.

The greatest prayer of all is 'Yes'. If I repeated this word in my heart, and ended up saying nothing else, I would have found a sure and certain way back to the Garden. 'Yes' represents my whole response to Jesus and to his message. There will always, of course, be room and need for prayers of petition, of repentance, and of gratitude. However, what I am suggesting is that my whole prayer-life can become under-laid with my constant and insistent whispers of 'Yes'. Calvary was Jesus saying 'Yes' to the Father, which completely neutralised the 'No' of Adam and Eve. When I put that drop of water in the chalice at the Offertory, I am joining my 'Yes' to Jesus, to his 'Yes' to the Father. At baptism somebody else said my 'Yes' for me, but now I must say it for myself.

God doesn't send me anywhere when I die. Rather he eternalises the direction in which I now choose to travel. The most important 'Yes' in my whole life is my 'Yes' of now. When I die, God eternalises that 'Yes' by embracing me into the fullness of life and love in the Trinity. 'Yes' is a powerfully significant prayer, because it betokens a decision, a choice. Jesus doesn't ask for discussions, but for decisions. God is totally a God of *now*, and the only 'yes' in my whole life that he's interested in is my 'yes' of *now*. That 'yes' rules out every 'no' that preceded it. I cannot think of a more healthy or life-giving mantra than to just constantly repeat the word 'yes'. The greatest 'yes' of all, of course, is the 'yes' to death, when it comes. Having said 'yes' all my life, it shouldn't be surprising to find that that final 'yes' is very simple indeed.

Space suggests that I bring this chapter to an end. I have very little to add, really. What is important to remember is that there is no end to the little whispers of prayer that fly like arrows to-wards the Lord. Take your pick of whatever word comes to your heart. *Thanks. Praise you, Lord. Holy, Holy.* I learned to walk by walking, and to talk by talking; and so I will become completely immersed in this form of praying by practising it. It is a road to many wonders, a path of many miracles. To watch the Jews at the Wailing Wall in Jerusalem, or to watch a group of Muslims in a Mosque, one must be struck by the repetitious nature of their prayer … repeating the same words again and again. I like to imagine Jesus praying this way.

As I said before, there are many ways of praying, but I offer you this one as one that really has been a great source of blessing for me. Like anything else, it becomes easier, and more automatic with practice. It is the way of developing a praying heart, where prayer under-girds my every activity. All the other activities and areas of my day must surely be blessed by this accompani-ment. 'I'll walk with God from this day on.' Whispering my mantra is one way of walking with God, of 'learning to live and to walk in the Spirit'. Such prayer becomes as much part of me as my breathing, which, most of the time, I am not aware of.

You find yourself waking up at night with a mantra in your heart. There is no reason to accept that our hearts cannot continue to pray even when we're asleep. I don't pretend to understand the dynamics of this, but I have good reason for believing it. Once we venture down this path of prayer, the Spirit can lead us anywhere, or to any possibilities there are. I bring goodwill, and I offer my readiness and willingness to travel, and the Spirit will do all the rest.

Forever and always

God is *constant*. In other words, he is the same yesterday, today, and always. A constant could be represented by a straight line. God is not a graph, moving from highs to lows on different dates, and on different occasions. Naturally, the only experience we have is our own. This experience of ourselves, how we function, think, feel, or reason, is bound to limit our ability to understand and grasp anything that is greater than us. We are human, and heirs to all that is human. We are in a process, an on-going state of evolution, a state of constant change. We experience this mostly through our moods, our humours, and our feelings. We are emotional creatures, and we must not forget that 'motion' and 'emotion' are expressions of the same thing.

One of my happier memories of childhood was travelling to Dublin on the train. The whole world was a wonder as I watched everything flying by. I was particularly struck by the telephone and electricity wires. My head moved in unison with them, as they dipped, and were lifted again at the next pole. It was years later when I discovered that life can be a bit like that. It is as if there were some sort of gravity pull that drags us down, until we regain control of things, and get back on an even keel again. Life is a dynamic, always in motion. If I am not moving forward, then, I can be sure that I'm moving backwards.

To live is to change, and to live life well is to have changed often (Cardinal Newman). It is not possible for the human mind to gasp the concept of something that is constant, in season, and out of season. Even the Pyramids of Egypt are constantly being repaired against erosion. There is not a cell in my body that was there seven years ago. We are constantly grower bigger, sometimes wider, and always older.

Because God is constant, whatever his plan was in creation, we can be sure that it has not changed. God is Love, and he could never be anything else. It is God's essence and nature to love 100%. He created us to share his love with us, and to have us reflect some of his own attributes. In other words, he made us in his image and likeness. Imagine taking a mirror off a wall, shattering it on the ground, and then handing a piece of that mirror to each of a group of people. Each person possesses a part of the mirror. It is as if each person reflects some different aspect of God. No one person possesses all of the mirror, or the complete picture. It is together that we can unite as one, and reflect the face of God. That is why Jesus prayed, 'Father, may they be one in us, as you are in me, and I am in you.' 'By this will everybody know that you are my disciples, if you have love, one for another.' When God creates, he provides what is needed for that creature to live as he had intended in his creation. All of nature obeys the seasons. Very soon, the daffodils will be out again. The birds will begin to migrate again. The days will begin to get longer, and the weather will begin to get warmer. God's creation provides for these things to happen. He doesn't create something and then abandon it to its own devices. It is all part of an extraordinary pattern, and the order and evidence of this pattern reflects the order and glory of God.

I remember seeing a poster some time ago. It was of a cat, lying down, looking at me. The caption read 'Does God seem far away? Guess who moved!' God's plan is love, love, love all the way. Jesus said, 'They who see me, see the Father, and they who hear me, hear the Father who sent me.' It is very important for us to remember that central point. When we look at Jesus in the gospels, we are looking at God in action. It was God who had pity on the widow of Naim, and raised her son to life again. It was God who wept at the tomb of Lazarus, or who wept over Jerusalem, because they rejected his love. His tears at the tomb of Lazarus were not tears of despair, but tears of empathy for his friends Martha and Mary. It mattered nothing if the person was a pagan, a Samaritan, a prostitute, a tax collector, or an untouchable leper. If they stopped him, they were healed. There was no distinction between Jew or Gentile. God has no grandchildren; we are all children of God.

The whole gospel could be summarised in the story of the Prodigal Son. Remember, this story never happened. It was a story that Jesus used to teach us something very important about the Father. This son hit Skid Row with a vengeance. To the Jews, pigs were unclean, and must not be approached under any condition. The son in the story ended up feeding pigs. He reached the nadir of his decadence when he sank so low that he was willing to eat the food provided for the pigs. That was his 'bottom', to use a phrase that would be familiar to recovering alcoholics. The lesson of the story, of course, is that the Father stood with open arms to welcome him home, and he went to great lengths to celebrate that event. It is not possible to exagerate God's love for us. In *Bread That Is Broken* (Van Breeman), we are told that 'the saint is not the person who loves God, but the person who is convinced that God loves her'. St John says, 'In this is love, not that we love God, but that God first loved us.' To quote Van Breeman again: 'Faith is to have the courage to accept God's acceptance.'

Annie was in a Hospice dying of cancer. I was with her on a Friday evening. I had to go away for the weekend, and I had reason to believe that Annie would not be alive when I returned on Monday. I prayed with her, gave her Absolution, and anointed her with oil. I held her hands as I spoke to her. 'Annie, pet, I don't know, but God might come looking for you at the weekend when I'm away. If he does come, I want you to know that your bags are packed and you're ready to go.' I looked her straight in the eye, and asked her, 'Sure you won't be afraid to meet him?' Her answer was instant: 'Father, I'm sure he's going to be very happy to see me!' (Yes, her body was in the mortuary when I returned on Monday.)

The Prodigal Son had a problem accepting the Father's love. He couldn't accept the fact that the Father was ready and willing to restore him to his place as the older member of the family. He just asked to be accepted as a hired servant, because he didn't think himself worthy of anything else. This is an obvious and frequent mistake to make. We forget that *God loves us because he is good,* totally irrespective of whether we are good or bad. I could summarise what I'm trying to say here by stating that I am really happy to be judged by God when I die ... I wouldn't trust people at all!

There's a scene in the gospel that has its own little twist of humour. It seems Peter is beginning to get the 'hang' of what Jesus is all about, so he throws in a question just to test that his impressions are correct. 'How many times should I forgive my brother? Seven times?' Peter was being really generous in suggesting seven times, because, surely three or four times was more than enough. Imagine his surprise to be told, 'Not seven times, but seventy times seven times.' Wow! In the language of the day, seventy times seven times was one way of expressing something that was endless, a number that was outside all the boundaries. That shook Peter, just as it should shake us.

However, it is important to remember that I'm not speaking here about what we should do. Rather I am speaking of how God understands love and forgiveness. 'To err is human; to forgive is divine.' When Jesus called Peter, we are told that 'Jesus looked at Peter'. Later on, after Peter denied him, we are told again, 'And Jesus turned and looked at Peter.' That shook Peter to his foundations because he saw that the look hadn't changed one bit. The love and acceptance was still there. That is why Peter could write, 'Always have an answer ready to give to those who ask you the reason for the hope that you have'.

There were two others crucified with Jesus on Calvary. They both probably deserved to end up as they did. Certainly one of them admitted that they deserved their fate. This one may never have said a prayer in his life. He may never have gone to a synagogue, and he may have treated others with great selfishness and greed. However, right there at the very end of his life, he turned to Jesus, asked for help, and was promised heaven that very day. It's never too late for God!

I baptised a baby some time ago. A beautiful healthy baby, very much welcomed by parents, family and friends. Both parents came from quite extended families, so the church was fairly full for the occasion. I walked up and down in front of the people, with baby Carol in my arms. I told them that she was the most important and the most loved person in that church that day, and she wasn't doing a thing to merit any of that. All she had to do was to be, just to exist, to be present. I spoke to her parents on her behalf: 'You wanted me. You have me, and now you had better look after me, because I could never manage on my own.' I told them how wonderful it would be if she could carry this into life with her, in her relationship and attitude towards God. 'You wanted me. You created me. Therefore, you will just have to look after me, because I could never manage on my own.' To know that she is loved by God by just existing, by just being, and not trying to earn it, or to meet some self-imposed expectation of a God that has never existed; that, indeed would be a wonderful gift. She received many presents on the day of her baptism, but this didn't cause her the slightest concern! Later on, she will strive to repay, to reciprocate, to 'get even' for the goodness of others, because life will teach her that there are really no free lunches. There's no such thing as Santa Claus!

We are all familiar with the story of God's creation in the Garden. What I am saying here is that the Garden is still on offer. Jesus ran after us, touched us on the shoulder, and whispered, 'The Father sent me to tell you that he wants you to return to the Garden, where he has a big hug waiting for you.' That message is at the kernel of the gospels. Jesus even offers himself as a guide to bring us home, because 'No one can come to the Father except through me.' That welcome hug was there even for the Prodigal Son, who had walked away from his father's love, and chose to go his own way. What wonderful good news it is to know that the Garden is there for us, and the welcome hug awaits us.

Jesus complained that 'the sin of this world is unbelief in me'. 'When the Son of Man comes will he find any faith on this earth?' On top of what I have just stated, I would go one step further, and say that the Garden is *now*. Some years ago in the US there was a television programme that was based on some

47

sort of organised chaos. One of the items had four people in a supermarket with empty trolleys. The whistle blew, and they were off at full speed, grabbing all they could from the shelves on either side. When the whistle blew a second time, they made their way to the check-out. Each had mixed emotions. 'Oh, I never saw that. I should have taken more of those, etc.' The goods of each person were checked, and the person with the highest value of goods was declared the winner.

Just imagine the following scenario: I get a committed Christian and I put him in the show with his own trolley. He is in no hurry. He picks up a loaf of bread, and heads down to the butter section. Then he makes his way across for a pint of milk, meanwhile picking up, and replacing items that fell from one of his competitor's trolley. When they get to the check-out he immediately becomes the focus of attention, derisive laughter, and cynical comment. 'What on earth are you about?' one of them asked. 'Did nobody tell you about the competition? What are you smiling for anyhow?' The man turned to the questioner and quietly replied 'Actually, my Father owns the supermarket! A loaf of bread, a pound of butter, and a pint of milk is all I need for today. I'll be back to-morrow.'

There is nothing I will get when I die that I'm not offered now. The road to heaven is heaven. In the next few insights, I intend looking at how damaged and fragile our human nature is. This will lead us on to look at what Jesus has done to set things right again, and make it possible for us to return to our former glory. Of course, of ourselves, we are not 'ready-made material' for heaven! Any claim, right, or entitlement we have is totally and completely as a direct result of the salvation earned for us through the death and resurrection of Jesus. Before we even consider what Jesus has done for us, it would be good to be ready and willing to put our hand in his, and let him lead us home. That is the greatest and the only thanks he asks for.

Damaged goods

A source of some of our problems is a failure to make a clear distinction between God and ourselves. God made us in his image, but we run the risk of returning the compliment, and making God in our image! It would be a disaster to confuse the Creator with the creature.

A sister of mine bought a new computer some time ago, and, by the nature of things, she is quite dependent on it, and makes good and constant use of it. Unfortunately, her computer is proving to be a 'lemon'. It seems to be 'crashing' on a regular basis. Immediately this happens, she is on the phone to the suppliers. There is no way she would attempt to open it up, check out the cards or the mother board, or use cello tape or superglue! When you and I are in need of renewal, we must always return to the Creator, who alone can do for us what we never could do for ourselves.

It is important to make a few clear distinctions early on here. When I speak of us being damaged, I speak of sin. However, when I speak of sin, I am not thinking of anything we do. Sin is something that was committed against us. We are the victims of sin, Original Sin. Because of this we are fundamentally damaged, with a hole in the ozone layer of our souls that only the Creator can recreate. 'Behold I make all things new.' This is not a question of cello tape or superglue. The result of this damage is that we are left with some sort of basic rebelliousness and, no matter how much God loves us; no matter how often we are reminded of that, or no matter in how many and varied ways God expresses his love for us, there is a tendency in us to do things our way.

If I hold a bunch of keys in my hand, hold out my hand, and open it, I can be sure that the keys will fall to the ground. There is a force of gravity at work, and it is the stuff of magicians to give the illusion that the keys are suspended in the air, and even begin to rise higher! 'I did it my way', 'Going my way' are more than just the titles of a movie or a song. Original sin is no longer original. In our different ways we have inherited the pride and stubbornness of Adam and Eve, and it can go against the grain to obey.

It really does come down to a question of obedience. Jesus was clear and constant in describing his own mission as 'doing the will of him who sent me'. 'If you love me, you will obey me,' he tells us. Original sin was caused by a refusal to obey, and obedience is the only antidote or antibiotic for such a sin. The problem really arises out of the fact that we know what to do. God's law is written in our hearts. No matter how much some people try to hide it, or deny it, each of us has a conscience. One look at a child of three, and you know he's been 'up to something'!

A stone cannot change its substance and become a flower. Similarly, we cannot lift ourselves out of the quicksand of our own selfishness. We are in a human condition, subject to the law of gravity, which will prevent us, of our own accord, from rising above that condition. We are 'infected' with the three evils of sin, sickness, and death, none of which was part of God's original creation. These are the weeds in the field of good wheat that Jesus speaks about, and it was not the farmer or his workforce who sowed them.

A man went to his doctor one time, and he was really worried. He told the doctor that every part of his body that he touched was really sore. The doctor gave him a thorough examination, and an e-ray. He returned the following day for the results, and was dreading the news he might receive. He asked the doctor if he had found out what was wrong with him, and the doctor said he had. When he asked what it was, the doctor told him 'Your finger's broken'! Once the man discovered what was wrong with him, he realised that the rest of him was ok! It's very important for us to know, and to understand 'what's wrong with us'.

This is not any kind of put-down or guilt trip. It's simply a question of knowing the truth, and accepting that truth. 'The truth will set you free.'

One of my earliest memories of growing up was watching my mother make bread. Practice had brought it to a fine art, and she never had to measure anything. I was one of a large family, so the bowl she used was the largest she had. In went the flour, the baking soda, the baking powder, and the buttermilk. What excited me most was when she got to the raisins. She was generous with these and, after the stirring was over, the dough was turned out on a large timber block. Her hands worked vigorously, as she kneaded that dough into a soft pliable ball. Out came the rolling pin, and the dough was then levelled out flat, about an inch or two in depth. She then took a large tumbler, turned it upside down and, dipping it in dry flour, she proceeded to make scones.

Let us stop the process here for a moment. If that ball of dough represented human nature, it should have a health warning on it! The raisins represent the weaknesses that are inherent in our nature; they are part of what we are. Then each of the scones represents each one of us, each of us with our own unique collection of weaknesses. No two scones possess the same raisins, nor would the number in each be the same. Identical twins could have completely different human weaknesses. One could become a chronic alcoholic, while the other could still have his confirmation pledge and, who knows, but he may still have his First Communion money!

Let us take the example of alcohol. A man could take his first drink on his seventieth birthday, and be hospitalised for severe alcoholism on his seventy-first. The chemistry or metabolism of his body is such that alcohol becomes an allergy that breaks down the whole fibre of his being. Alcoholism is a physical allergy, and a mental addiction. His brother could get sick at the very smell of alcohol. The point I am trying to make here is that we all have our own unique personal collection of weaknesses, and none of us can throw a stone at another. 'There, but for the Grace of God, go I'. Being convinced of my human condition is essential for salvation. Not much point in speaking about a Saviour to those who do not accept that they need one!

There are two things that can help clarify this for us. The first is that the gospels are *now*; they are not a history of something that happened in the past. The second point is that I am every person in the gospel. I have my own blindness, my own dumbness, and my own demons. There are many forms of blindness and many kinds of demons. Physical blindness is very obvious to the blind person, and to those around. The other forms of blindness are much more difficult to detect and, indeed, the person effected is probably the last one to be aware of it. One of the problems with alcoholism, for example, is that it is the only sickness known to medicine that, by its nature, denies its own existence. In other words, the alcoholic himself is the last person to become aware of his problem. The secret is to be able and willing to name, claim, and tame my demons. To throw the doors and windows of my heart wide open, and invite the Spirit to enter and reveal the truth to me. 'He will convict you of sin,' says Jesus.

It is difficult, if not impossible for us to comprehend just how weak our human condition is. My weaknesses are part of who I am, and I could cut off a leg sooner than remove a weakness. Even if I did sever a leg, my weaknesses are still there, because they are more part of me than my leg. St Paul had a good grasp of his condition, and it is worth listening to him at some length to help us understand. 'We know that the law is spiritual, but I am full of human weaknesses, sold as a slave to sin. I cannot explain what is happening to me, because I do not do what I want, but, on the contrary, the very things I hate. Well then, if I do the evil I do not want to do, I agree that the law is good; but in this case, I am not the one striving towards evil, but it is sin, living in me. I know that nothing good lives in me, I mean, in my flesh. I can want to do what is right, but I cannot do it. In fact I do not do the good I want, but the evil I hate. Therefore, if I do the evil I do not want to do, I am not the one striving towards evil, but sin which is within me. I discover then this reality: though I wish to do something good, the evil within me asserts itself first. My inmost self agrees and rejoices with the law of God, but I notice in my body another law challenging the law of the spirit, and delivering me as a slave to the law of sin written in my members. Alas for me! Who will free me from this condition linked to death?' (Rom 7: 14-24). Paul then goes on to thank Jesus for changing everything for him. Paul captures very well that basic rebelliousness that is within all of us.

People caught in addictions to drugs or sexual perversions are only too well aware of just how impossible it is for us to fight and conquer our human weaknesses. 'Lord, give me the serenity to accept the things I cannot change.' When it comes to dealing with our human condition, the first thing we have to do is stop playing God. God becomes God in my life the moment I get out of the way, and let him take over. The secret of gaining human freedom is through surrender. Pure religion won't do it. Religion is what we do, it has to do with rules and regulations, it is external, and it is about control. Spirituality, on the other hand, is internal, it is about what God does in us, and it is about surrender. If a religious person is typified by the Pharisees, then a religious person is perfect, and has no need of God to do anything for him. The Pharisee in the Temple stood up and told God all the great and good things he was doing and, instead of saying 'Praise the Lord', he might have said 'Praise me, Lord.' In the meantime, there is another man, a publican, a person of much lower rank in the social and religious scale, and he knelt at the back of the Temple, lowered his head and whispered, 'Oh God, be merciful to me, a sinner.' 'That man,' said Jesus, 'is the one who went home justified.'

One simple understanding and definition of holiness is to become convinced that I am a greater sinner than I ever thought I was. The virtue in this is that, once that happens, I drop that stone from my fist, I stop looking down on others, and I leave all judgements to God. Have you ever noticed that, in the Mass, we use the word 'I' three times in all ... 'I confess ... that I have sinned ... Lord, I am not worthy.' All the rest is plural but, when it comes to sin, you speak for yourself, and leave the rest of us alone! There are two conditions for getting to heaven: first, to be a sinner, and second, to admit that fact. The blind, the lame, and the lepers didn't pretend to be anything other than what they were, and Jesus could work miracles for them. We cannot fail to be struck by the fact that, after all Jesus said about becoming like little children, he should discover that his apostles were arguing about which of them was the greatest. Indeed, his apostles had their weaknesses, and Jesus accepted them as they were. All he asked was that they be prepared to admit to those weaknesses, and not allow them destroy love, or damage relationships. 'Peter, do you love me more than these?', which could be paraphrased as, 'Peter, do you still think that you are better than any of these?'

Jesus was betrayed, denied, and deserted by his apostles, but Judas was the only one who considered himself as being beyond redemption, and outside the pale of Jesus' love and acceptance. Jesus would never want Judas to die by suicide but, because of freewill, he couldn't stop him.

One final word. My weaknesses play a very important role in my spiritual growth. If God offered me perfection right now, I would turn it down completely. There is nobody perfect but God and, without my weaknesses, and the struggles they present to me, I would be deprived of compassion, empathy, and all kinds of human understanding of other people. Without my weaknesses there would be no need, or no evidence of God's power working in me. The Pharisees were convinced that God needed them more than they needed him.

St Paul, having spoken of some wonderful spiritual experiences he had, goes on to tell us, 'Lest I become proud after so many and extraordinary revelations, I was given a thorn in my flesh, a true messenger of Satan, to slap me in the face. Three times I prayed to the Lord that it leave me, but he answered "My grace is enough for you; my great strength is revealed in weakness." Gladly, then, will I boast of my weakness, that the strength of Christ may be mine. For when I am weak, then I am strong'. The miracle of salvation is how God can 'turn all things into good.' I can be a much more compassionate person today because of my failures, and the only value the past has are the lessons it taught me. If my weaknesses convince me that I need a Saviour, then they are a direct source of goodness, and a forceful influence in my salvation.

Referring back to the dough in my mother's baking, Jesus took on *all* of the raisins, and he showed that the power of the Spirit within was much more powerful than all of the weaknesses put together. He then gives us the Spirit that was within him, plus the scone with whatever weaknesses each one of us has. He just asks us to believe that his Spirit is more than enough to overcome whatever weaknesses we have. St John says, 'Little children, there is a Spirit within you that will overcome any evil spirit you meet on the road of life.'

A Saviour and a Redeemer

The whole story of salvation is based on human weakness. It is a story of God coming to meet us where we are, as we are. He could have loved us from a distance, but he decided to come among us and, to go much further, as he knelt at the apostles' feet with a basin of water and a towel. This was really accepting them at ground level, as it were.

There is a legend about God, the Great Composer of the Universe, and the wonderful and beautiful harmonious music that he wrote through his creation. He shared out each section of the orchestra to different sections of his creation. To the birds, he entrusted the pan pipes, and to the elephants he entrusted the bugles and the trumpets. The grasses were entrusted with the string music, and the clouds and the seas took on the role of percussion. Each section of his creation had a pivotal role to play in producing the heavenly harmony of God's creation. When it came to humans, however, God made a special decision. Because they were gifted with reason, and with common sense, God decided that they would know what harmonised and what didn't. He decided to trust them to know what belonged and what didn't belong in this harmony of creation. And so, the music began. The harmony was, literally, out of this world. Each section of the orchestra made a wonderful and vital contribution, and this contributed enormously to the beauty of the whole. This went on for some time and, indeed, it was unthinkable that it should ever end. Then one day, completely out of the blue, the worst possible scenario happened. In the midst of the harmony there was a screech, a roar, and a frightening unharmonious note that resounded throughout the universe. Every section of the orchestra came to a sudden stop. 'What was that?' whispered the birds. 'It was humans,' replied the wind. 'They have rebelled, refused to follow the harmony, and they want to do things their way.' 'What will happen now?' asked the clouds.

'Will God scrap the whole score, and bring it all to an end?' The various possibilities of what God might do were discussed among different sections of the orchestra. However, all of them were off the mark. What did God decide to do? He reached out into the universe, and took hold of that one discordant note and, using that as his theme, he wrote a completely new score, based entirely on that one discordant note. And that, my friend, is the story of God's salvation, that is provided for us through Jesus Christ. Our brokenness, our failures, our human weaknesses provide the foundation on which God builds the whole economy of salvation. Another way of saying this is, if we had not failed, then Jesus would not have come.

A brief note on freewill, before we go any further, because it is vital that we grasp this concept if we are to understand how God deals with us. To do a good, presumes that I must have a choice of not doing the good, or of doing the evil; otherwise there is no merit in being good. An atheist cannot believe in something being good or bad, unless there is something or Somebody there to make it so. An atheist cannot believe in free-will. Freewill is a vast question, because we cannot be considered morally responsible human beings unless we have free-will. Without freewill there is no love, no wrong-doing, and all personal relationships are simply forms of manipulation. It is important to remember that we can make choices, we can make decisions. That is why, in creation, God could not possibly create human beings who are programmed in such a way that they could never sin, or turn their backs on him. Adam and Eve were totally free to walk away, from the moment God created them. Jesus came to invite us back to the Garden; not to drag us, goose-step us, or blackmail us into obedience. Jesus invites us, and every invitation has RSVP written at the bottom of it. Not to reply is itself a reply.

In Jesus, the Creator had come to recreate. Apart from Calvary itself, the mission of Jesus is best seen when he was baptised in the river Jordan. John the Baptist had been calling on sinners to come out to the Jordan, acknowledge their sins, and be baptised in the waters for the forgiveness of those sins. Jesus, of course, was the sinless one, the spotless Lamb of God. However, after thirty years of schooling in the Spirit, and spending nights all alone listening to the Father, he was ready to take on his mission.

John was shocked when Jesus showed up at the Jordan river, and he protested that it was Jesus who should be baptising him, rather than the other way around. Jesus spoke quietly and firmly to John, in such a way that John realised that there was a special reason for this, even if he didn't understand. Jesus told him that he would understand at a later time. And so Jesus went down into the river with the burden of *all* of our sins on his shoulders. The burden would have been too much for him, did not the Father and the Spirit come to his rescue. 'As soon as he was baptised, Jesus came up from the water, and he saw the Spirit of God come down like a dove and rest on him. At the same time a voice from heaven said "This is My Son, the Beloved; he is My Chosen One".' Jesus came up out of that river with the power of God within, and the burden of human weaknesses on his shoulders.

His life would clearly show that the power of God could overcome all of our human weaknesses, with particular reference to sin, sickness, and death. These were not part of God's creation. Jesus told a story about a farmer who sowed good wheat in his field. When the wheat came up, the servants noticed that weeds began to appear as well. They went to the farmer and asked him, 'Was that not good wheat that you sowed in that field? Where did the weeds come from?' 'An enemy (the name Satan means enemy) has done this.' 'Do you want us to pull up the weeds?' the servants asked. 'Oh no,' said the farmer, 'I will do that myself because, in pulling up the weeds, you might pull up the wheat as well.' Jesus came to remove those weeds because we could not do this ourselves.

I never believe that I could do much about sickness and death, but part of my earlier understanding of the spiritual journey was that I was responsible for removing all of the other weeds. We were provided with many instruments that were supposed to do just that, like the Particular Examen, penances, fasting, and other forms of self-denial. Even the word 'self-denial' is suspect because it includes that word 'denial'. Thank God those things didn't work, because we all would have been perfect by our thirtieth birthday!

As soon as Jesus was baptised he headed out into the desert, where Satan was waiting to test him. Up till now Satan had a free run. Jesus called him 'The Prince of this world'. He brought Jesus up to a high mountain and offered him the kingdoms of the earth if he would adore him. Those kingdoms were Satan's to give, before Jesus came to set up his kingdom, and to proclaim his victory over the kingdom of Satan. Jesus declared war on the kingdom of Satan and, whenever he came across a person in Satan's control, he released that person. Satan did everything within his power to thwart the plans of Jesus. He even proclaimed Jesus as the Messiah, in the hope that this would cause a riot, and things might get out of control.

When Jesus set his face towards Calvary, Peter tried to persuade him not to go; but Jesus recognised that Peter was only being used, and he said, 'Get behind me, Satan!' Jesus made it abundantly clear that he came in search of the lost, and all those who knew they could never make it alone.

The stories he used are poignant and beautiful. He was a brilliant teacher, who brought people from the known to the unknown. His listeners were all familiar with sheep and shepherds, and how they interrelated with each other. If a man had one hundred sheep and one went astray, he would leave the ninety-nine, search for the lost one; and when he finds it, he brings it back to the flock with great joy. Jesus said that he came for the lost sheep of the House of Israel. He said he had a mission to accomplish, and he could never be at peace until it was completed. He made it very clear, again and again, that he came to save, and not to condemn.

His treatment of the woman about to be stoned to death is very touching. When Jesus was surrounded by Pharisees in one

of their houses, another such woman was so sure of his acceptance that she walked in right in front of everyone, and knelt at
his feet, and began crying. That caused some stir among the onlookers, but Jesus used the occasion to great advantage, clearly
showing, once again, the whole purpose of his mission. To understand the extraordinary nature of such an event, one would
have to see it through the eyes of those who watched on. They
were totally shell-shocked. It was unthinkable what Jesus was
allowing to happen to him. He couldn't possibly be a prophet,
because a prophet would know what kind of woman she was,
and would have nothing whatever to do with her. In fact, it is
true to say that the woman herself would have nothing to do
with prophets, because she had good reason to fear them, and
anybody that represented them.

If Jesus were on this earth for three minutes, instead of thirty-
three years, he could have summarised his whole message in the
Story of the Prodigal Son. There are three significant persons in
the story, the Prodigal, his begrudging jealous brother, and the
forgiving father. Any one of us can be the Prodigal or his brother
at different times in our lives, and Jesus is calling us to become
the forgiving father. The father's role is to reconcile the two ele-
ments within all of us, the sinner and the self-righteous. Guilt is
not from God. Satan is called 'the accuser of our brothers. He ac-
cuses them day and night before our God.' To err is human, and
to forgive is divine. Right up to his last breath Jesus was there
with total forgiveness. It is never too late for God. One of those
crucified with him may never have turned to God in his life, but,
right there, he asked for help, and was promised heaven that
very day. 'Something beautiful, something good; all my confu-
sion he understood. All I had to offer him was brokenness and
strife, but he made something beautiful of my life.'

This man was in jail, awaiting execution. It was in a place
where executions were carried out in public. One morning he
heard people gather in the square above. The noise grew louder
as the numbers increased, and the man had good reason to think
that his day had come. His name was Barabbas; his trial was a

showpiece, and his death was inevitable. As the noisy crowd gathered, he crouched in a corner, waiting for the steps of the soldiers coming to get him. The noise above increased, and there was much shouting. This went on for some long time. Finally, as far as he could make out, the crowd seemed to have moved away. There was silence. Then he heard the footsteps. So it was his day after all. The door was opened, and two soldiers stood in the doorway. One of them beckoned, and said 'Ok, get out of here!' Barabbas didn't move. 'Get out of here and go home', one of them roared at him. There was no way that Barabbas was prepared to move, because he was convinced it would be a case of 'being shot while trying to escape'. One of the soldiers grabbed a hold of him, dragged him through the open door, and dropped him there. Then they both walked away. When Barabbas felt it was safe to do so, he slipped over behind a wall nearby. He crouched down and waited for the slightest sound. Eventually, he heard voices. He peeped over the wall, and saw people make their way back from the country. He kept out of sight, only venturing the occasional peep around the side of the wall. Finally, he saw someone he knew, and he called him in a whisper. The man came towards him, and joined Barabbas behind the wall. The man was amazed that Barabbas hadn't been told what had happened. He persuaded Barabbas that it was quite safe for him to walk in public again, because he was now a free man. He brought Barabbas out the country, and showed him three crosses on a distant hill. 'Do you see that middle cross?' he asked. 'Well, that was the one intended for you. But that man Jesus, he took your place, and you are now free; so, if you take my advice, get out of here while the going is good.' Thank you, Jesus.

Completing his work

Think of the Trinity as a triangle. The Father is at the top, with Jesus and the Spirit at either corner at the bottom. The sides of the triangle are like two arms stretching out to embrace us, and draw us to the Father's eternal hug. 'That we might live no longer for ourselves, but for him, Jesus sent the Holy Spirit as *his first gift to those who believe, to complete his work on earth, and bring us the fullness of grace.'*

When Jesus returned to the Father, he brought his body with him. When the Spirit came, he would need a body, and that's where we come in. An evil spirit needs somebody's hand to plant the bomb, and somebody's tongue to tell the lie. If the Holy Spirit is to speak, he needs our voices. If he is to heal the sick, he needs our hands. We do not have to do anything beyond providing the body, and allowing the Holy Spirit work through us. Mary, our Mother, didn't actually do anything; rather she submitted to the Spirit and allowed him use her in any way he chose. There are two parts to the story of salvation, i.e. what Jesus has done, and how we allow the Spirit in us respond to all of that. 'It is his blood and our faith,' St Paul tells us.

Faith is one of the gifts of the Spirit. When Jesus walked on this earth, he was Saviour, forgiving sins, healing the sick, and giving hope to those in darkness and in the shadow of death. He was not Lord yet, because he did not have the victory yet. It was only when he returned in triumph to his Father that he could give the Spirit, and proclaim the permanent establishment of his kingdom.

There is nothing automatic about God. Nothing happens in us until we say 'Yes', be that for good or for evil. Our freewill is paramount, and neither the Father, the Son, nor the Spirit will over-ride or bypass that in any way. In simple English, I have to say 'yes' to the Spirit so that I will be given the grace to say 'yes' to what Jesus has done for me. Only then will 'salvation come to my house today.' The Spirit takes over where Jesus laid off. When Jesus rose from the dead on Easter morn, nothing happened to anybody else. The apostles would have run away all over again that very evening, if there was any pressure put on them. They had to wait for their Easter, which is what we call Pentecost. Just as the stone was rolled away from the front of the tomb and Jesus came out into resurrected life, so the doors of the Upper Room would be flung open, and the apostles would come out into their resurrected life.

The third part of this story is when the doors of our hearts are flung open, and we are born again into a new and eternal life. As I said in an earlier chapter, the terminus is Pentecost, and it would be a mistake to get off the train too early. 'Stay in Jerusalem, and don't leave till the Spirit comes,' were among the final words of Jesus. Knowing the apostles as he did, Jesus knew that they would surely get it wrong all over again. As a Christian, I have nowhere to go, and I cannot go forward without the presence of the Spirit within. The Spirit is like the petrol or the diesel in a car. Without petrol or diesel the car will move, but I'll have to push it. In the beginning God took clay, and he breathed his Spirit into it. Clay, on its own, can do nothing, and is of no use whatever. Without heat or water, nothing can grow in it. *Humus* is the Latin word for clay, and we are human, i.e. we are made of clay. *Humilitas* is the Latin for 'of the ground' and, on our own, there is no way that we could ever raise ourselves above that level.

By myself I do not have what it takes to be a Christian. Chesterton says that we never actually become Christian; we are always *in the process of becoming*. When the Spirit came upon Mary, Jesus was formed within her. That same Spirit must come upon us, if the fullness of Jesus' salvation and redemption is to become a reality within us, and in our lives.

There once was a crow that looked very very unhealthy; eyes bloodshot, feathers falling off, and wings dragging in the mud. This drew the sympathy of a bunch of crows, who decided to approach him to see what they could do. The crow put on a brave face, and tried to pretend that all was well, but it was all in vain. Eventually, he decided to come clean, and unburden his problems. He felt that time was passing him by, and that he had fulfilled very few of the ambitions with which he set out in life. He was asked to name one such ambition. When he was promised confidentiality, he confessed that he always wanted to make a record. When asked what the record would contain, he bashfully replied 'Of me, singing'. This was too much for the other crows, who could not resist a snigger; something that deeply upset our friend, and brought a ringing retort. 'Why couldn't I sing? Did you ever hear a blackbird sing? Well I'm bigger than a blackbird, and the same colour, so why couldn't I sing like a blackbird? If you only knew all the trouble I've gone to to try and sing like a blackbird. I went to the health-shop. I bought wholegrain, Vivioptol, Ballygowan, and every kind of vitamin available. After all that, I went up on a tree, opened my mouth, and all that came out was "Caw! Caw!" I then decided to tape the blackbirds singing. I bought a C90 tape and went among the blackbirds, and filled it with blackbirds warbling. That would surely do it! I bought a walkman (brain bypass?) and, as I flew around or lay in bed at night, I had the headphones on, and the sounds of blackbirds singing were filling my brain. After all of that I flew up on a tree, opened my mouth, and, once again, it was "Caw! Caw!" (Author's note: Guys like me produce tapes because people like you buy them! The tape may help to change your thinking, which could lead to you changing your actions, but the tape won't do any of that for you!) ... back to the crow ... 'Then I got sheet music, and went for voice training, and really worked hard at it.' (Further note: The same applies to writing books and giving Retreats. They can help change your thinking but, of themselves, they won't change you!) ...back to the crow ...'After all of that I flew up on a tree, opened my mouth, and I still had my "Caw! Caw!" So, I hope you see now,' he said to the other crows, 'why I'm so depressed, and in such distress.' The other crows were speechless. What could one say? One by one they made some excuse about an appointment somewhere, and soon our friend was back on his own again. It was a long time later when the same group just happened to bump into each other. The other crows gathered around in amazement, spellbound at what they saw. The crow's feathers were shining, his eyes were sparkling, and he walked as if floating on air. 'What happened?' asked the others in amazement. 'Oh', said the crow, his face lighting up with a smile, 'you could never guess what happened. Shortly after the last time I met you, I was flicking through a newspaper. Something caught my eye in one corner, and I read it. It was about a surgeon in South Africa who did transplants. The idea hit me like a sledge hammer. A transplant! That's what I wanted all the time. How could I ever hope to sing like a blackbird if I didn't have the voice-box of a blackbird? I got the phone number of the surgeon, and I rang him straight away. He himself actually answered the phone. I told him about what I had read in the paper, and I asked him what kind of transplants he did. He rhymed off a few, like hearts, lungs, and livers. I asked him did he ever do a voice-box. He said "No", so I asked him would he be willing to do a voice-box. He said he certainly was willing, because it couldn't possibly be as complicated as a heart transplant. He agreed to take me on if I went out there. I flew to South Africa, and we kept in touch with all local hospitals and mortuaries, waiting for news about a dead blackbird (one with a donor card!). Eventually, my day came. I went down to that theatre completely at ease. I lay back on that table and let somebody else take over a problem that I was never going to resolve by myself. I ended up with the voice-box of a blackbird. The surgeon told me I would have to practise and, in time, I would get the hang of things. In no time at all I was up on a tree, singing my heart out, as beautiful as any blackbird. And now I discover that I cannot sing any other way. Oh, and by the way, one very important point. I have learned that the wholegrain, the Vivioptol, the vitamins, the C90 tape, the sheet music, the voice training ... not one penny of that money, or one minute of time was wasted, because if I had not done all those things, I would not be convinced now that they don't work!'

'I will take away your heart of stone, and give you a heart of flesh instead. I will breathe my Spirit into you, and you shall live,' says the Lord.

The Holy Spirit is the Breath, the Power of God. At the beginning of creation God breathed his Spirit into the clay, and a human being came into existence, a new life began. Jesus told Nicodemus that, to enter his kingdom, one had to be born again. 'Unless one is born again of water and the Holy Spirit, one cannot enter the kingdom of God. What is born of the flesh is flesh, and what is born of the Spirit is spirit.' The baptism of John the Baptist was that of water, which was for the forgiveness of sins. John spoke of one who would come after him who would baptise with water and with the Holy Spirit. This brings us to a point beyond sin; to a point of holiness, when we are anointed with the Spirit of God. Being anointed with the Spirit is the final and necessary part of our journey of salvation. We cannot respond to the offer of Jesus, nor can we avail of all that he gained for us, unless the Spirit within us makes that possible.

Original Sin is very pervasive, because, at any stage of the process, we can be tempted to take over, and try to complete the process ourselves. We have to imitate John the Baptist who knew that he had to decrease if Jesus were to increase. Instead of trying to take over, we should consciously make every effort to keep getting out of the way. As far as the Spirit is concerned, it is an on-going process of surrender. Those of us reared on religious practices could easily have a problem here, because of the emphasis that was put on what we *do*. As I said earlier, Mary didn't do anything. She yielded to the Spirit, and gave him a complete free hand to use her in any way he chose. She *magnified* the Lord, rather than magnify herself. She was the 'lowly servant' of the Lord, and she believed that there was nothing impossible for God, so she didn't feel any need to step in and do God's work for him. She is our role model *par excellance* when it comes to being open to the Spirit, and allowing the Spirit do all that he was sent to do.

Receiving the Spirit

We all have the Spirit of God within us; otherwise we would die, because God would recall his Spirit, and only the clay would remain. 'Dust thou art, and onto dust thou shalt return.' We have the Spirit, but the Spirit may not have us!

We can have the Spirit but lead very corporeal materialistic lives. We can have any kind of god we choose to invent, and we can get our power from money, pleasure, or status. There must be a very hollow ring to a life that is lived without God's Spirit. When the Spirit is absent or ignored, other spirits are more than ready to move in, and fill the vacuum. Not only is my life incomplete, but I myself am not complete unless I am filled with the Spirit of God.

Getting the Spirit is the simplest part of the process. 'Will the Father not surely give the Spirit to those who ask?' We speak about a 'release of the Spirit'. In other words, like the spring of living water at the core of the human heart, there is something blocking that Spirit, or that water, from gurgling up into a fountain within us. No matter how much water lies beneath the sand of a desert, an oasis is a rare sight. When we come to ask for the Spirit, it is important to remember that Jesus offered to send his Spirit long before anybody thought of asking him. In other words, it is very clearly the desire of Jesus that we should ask for, and receive his Spirit.

In the last few chapters, I have lined up my insights into some sort of coherent sequence. We have got to the point now where we have to stop *talking* about the Spirit, and prepare our hearts to *receive* that Spirit. At my baptism somebody else said 'yes' for me. It's now my turn to say my own 'yes'. Pentecost for me, or Annunciation for Mary, are interchangeable words. God has a special plan and purpose for each of us. That plan cannot begin until we say 'yes' to it, and accept the central truth that it is only by the power of God's Spirit that any of this can happen.

The biggest barrier to receiving the Spirit is the way the human mind works. We tend to filter everything through the mind, to make sense out of it first, to analyse it in the laboratory of our intelligence. The problem here is that we are approaching the whole thing from the wrong angle. It is not possible to make sense of the Spirit in our minds, nor is it possible to use our brains to unravel a mystery. Like the fountain of living water, the Spirit rises up from within a person. I experience it firstly, and come to understand it later, if at all.

I was speaking about the Spirit to a group of Sisters about thirty years ago. After that particular talk, I was having a cup of coffee in the parlour, when there was a knock on the door. A Sister entered the room, and I discovered later that she was 92 years of age. She looked at me with a serious childlike expression, and she blurted out, 'Father, whatever it is you're talking about, I want it, I want it all, and I want it now.' I nearly spluttered my coffee all over the place as I jumped to my feet. I took her by the arm, and I said, 'Come on, dear. We're going to the prayer-room, and I want you to say those self-same words to Jesus, because I'm sure he hasn't heard a prayer like that for a while.' We went to the prayer-room, and she blurted out, 'Jesus, whatever it is you're talking about, I want it, I want it all, and I want it now.' I laid my hands on her head, and I asked the Lord to fill her with his Spirit. I could almost hear the shell crack, as she began to cry. She cried her eyes out for quite a while, and I just sat there, and left her to it.

The following morning she came to me to tell about how she felt that night. She felt as if she was weightless, as she laughed and cried to herself all night. The following day was the last day of the Retreat. At the closing Mass I invited Sisters to share in the Prayers of the Faithful. Sr Peter's little voice got louder, and less crackly, as she prayed, 'Now thou dost dismiss thy servant in peace, O Lord, because my eyes have seen your salvation.' She died ten days later.

Her entry into Religious Life was a conversion. Thousands of conversions later, she came to the point of sheer simplicity where she could ask for 'all of whatever it is'! She had read many books, listened to many lectures, made many Retreats, etc. during her long life-time. At last, at 92 years of age, she was prepared to get down off her sycamore tree, and welcome the Spirit into her heart.

We are going to look at three different scenarios now, to help situate the actual receiving of the Spirit. The first happens when I celebrate Eucharist. If English was not my first language, or if I were newly ordained, I would not let that book on the altar out of my sight for a moment. If you are paying close attention to what is going on, and listening to the words, there is one thing you should notice. After the 'Holy Holy', I begin to say some prayers. Listen carefully, and you will notice a switch from saying prayers to reading a passage from the gospel. 'When they were at supper, he took bread, etc ... When supper was ended, he took the chalice ...' What's happening here is that I am actually reading the account in the gospels of what happened at the Last Supper. And, wait for it, the miracle of the Last Supper happens again right there in our presence.

The second scenario has to do with Pentecost. John XXIII, God bless him, asked the Lord for another, or a New Pentecost, because the church seemed to have lost the fire and enthusiasm of the first one. A group of people came together, not exactly sure what to pray for, but willing to do something about the Pope's wishes. They prayed quietly that the Spirit might come, not expecting anything very dramatic to happen. As they prayed, someone stood up, and read the account of the First Pentecost from the Acts of the Apostles. As the person read, everybody in the room was 'zapped' with a wonderful anointing of the Spirit, and Charismatic Renewal, as we know it, began in that room. The third scenario has to do with Mary and the Annunciation.

You imagine Mary as kneeling beside you, with her eyes closed, and her head slightly bowed. Watch her very carefully. Suddenly an angel of the Lord is standing there in front of her. She lifts her head, and clasps her hands in fear. She is looking straight at the angel. The angel spoke. 'Rejoice, full of grace, the Lord is with you.' Mary listened and was troubled at these words, wondering what this greeting could mean. But the angel said 'Do not fear, Mary, for God looked kindly on you. You shall conceive and bear a son, and you shall call him Jesus. He will be great, and shall rightly be called the Son of the Most High. The Lord God will give him the kingdom of David, his ancestor, and he will rule over the people of Jacob forever, and his reign shall have no end.' Then Mary said to the angel, 'How can this happen if I am a virgin?' And the angel said to her, 'The Holy Spirit will come upon you, and the power of the Most High will overshadow you; therefore, the holy child to be born shall be called Son of God ... For with God nothing is impossible'. Then Mary said, 'I am the servant of the Lord; let it be done to me as you have said.' It was at that moment that the Holy Spirit flooded Mary's soul, and the plan for our salvation was put into operation.

Let us look at that scene again, and make some changes. This time, you close your eyes, and Mary is watching you. The angel stands in front of you, and says those very same words to you. We are all called to form Jesus within us, so that, like Mary at the visitation, we can bring Jesus to those we meet. How can I do this? I get the same answer as Mary got, as I clearly hear the words, 'For there is nothing impossible for God.' Now the angel draws to one side, awaiting our answer. Nothing happens without my 'yes'. 'Yes, Lord, I want what you want. Please do with me whatever you wish to do. Knowing that the Spirit will never leave me, I am willing to be led by that Spirit in whatever direction you choose for me.' I whisper my 'yes' again and again. 'Be it done onto me according to your word'... again and again. I make that my only prayer of this day. I kneel beside Mary, and I join with her in saying 'yes'. I hand the Holy Spirit the key of willingness, allowing him free access to my mind, heart and soul.

A young woman who discovers that she is pregnant, and is delighted with the news, is the person who could best describe to me how to react at this stage. To sit and reflect on what has just happened; to let the whole thing sink in. To breathe deeply, and to be very conscious of the power of God's Breath within me. My thoughts are inner thoughts. I feel like Mary 'pondering the words within her heart'. What has happened is *real* and, like the young pregnant woman, I will become more and more aware of that as time goes by. I have hoisted the sails, and the gentle breeze of the Spirit is gently moving me out into the deep. The biggest consolation I have are the words of Jesus 'The Spirit will never leave you'. This Spirit will be there tomorrow and every day.

In the following chapter, I will speak about 'learning to live and to walk in the Spirit'. When a passenger ship comes within sight of New York, Southampton, or Cobh, it stops, and a pilot goes out in a tug boat, gets on board, and brings it into harbour. My days of rowing are over! I have surrendered to a Power greater than myself, and I am about to be guided out into uncharted waters, and to discover an inner Power that inspires my every thought and action. As well as getting a spring in my steps, I begin to experience the awakening of spring within, as new flowers break through to the surface. Like the crow, in an earlier story, I now can sing like a blackbird. I can identify with the apostles as they came out of that Upper Room. I wonder would they have had enough patience, hope, and trust to wait nine whole days for this to happen. The Spirit came because the Spirit was expected to come, and I feel certain that Mary's presence among them had a powerful effect on their sense of expectation. Elizabeth praised Mary, and said 'All these things happened to you because you believed that the promises of the Lord would be fulfilled.' When I ask for the Spirit ... *Come, Holy Spirit* ... then I can expect the Spirit to come.

Note: Gentle reader, do you believe/accept/feel that something has happened to you as you made your way through this chapter? Don't be in any hurry going on to the next chapter. Savour the moment. Breathe deeply of the Spirit. Think of that oasis in the desert. Experience that fountain of living water bubbling up within you. Now that you have read this chapter, you may have to go back and read it again, this time with prayer and reflection. The Holy Spirit is not confined to churches! He knows where you are, and only you can set limits to what he does in you. Open your mind, your heart, and your hands … and wait like Mary in the Upper Room. *It will happen exactly as you are told*, just as the shepherds found when they went to Bethlehem to see for themselves.

Living and walking

'Learn to live and to walk in the Spirit,' St Paul tells us. You have the Spirit; now let the Spirit have you. 'Little children, there is a power within you that is greater than any evil power you will meet on the road of life,' St John tells us. The Holy Spirit is like Popeye's spinach that can transform my greatest weaknesses into sources of strength. Nothing in my life will ever be the same again, once I learn to live and to walk in the Spirit. I am like the body, or the frame of a car into which the mechanic puts a brand new and powerful engine. I can move now, but I have to develop the constant habit of never moving, of never doing, of never acting without involving the Holy Spirit in the process. When I act in the power of the Spirit, I am free of Original sin, and I am free to return to the Garden, where I can walk with God in the cool of the evening.

Once I believe that I am saved, I begin to look saved, and my Christian witness begins. I cannot overemphasise the part the Spirit plays in this new way of living. Human nature being what it is, there is always the danger of welcoming the Spirit, being happy to have the Spirit, and then setting out on my own, as if nothing happened. The Spirit could be listed among my 'Emergencies Only' phone numbers! That can no longer be the case. You have only just begun to walk in the Spirit, and it is an on-going process to deepen that relationship, and allow the Spirit even greater freedom to work in you, and through you. It requires constant surrender, constant yielding, until I have handed over the whole initiative to the Spirit. If I am to be led by the Spirit, then I must accept that my role is to follow.

This directly confronts Original Sin, which was a decision to do things our way. It transforms our inner spirits into a humble and gentle obedience. We learn to listen to the gentle breeze that is the Spirit, and to allow that breeze to fill our sails as we float along. I am no longer in control, but have totally surrendered to a Higher Power. Like Mary after the Annunciation, Jesus is beginning to be formed in me. In other words, I become more Christ-like, developing a family resemblance to Jesus, as a member of the family of God. Might I suggest a little prayer that I believe can help? Just to constantly whisper, 'Spirit and Breath and Power of God.' Nothing more. Just a constant reminder again and again, because it is so easy for us to forget, and get caught up in all the troubles and travails of life again. There can be no going back. If I say my daily 'yes', the Spirit will continue to lead me forward. The work is not complete yet, until, to quote St Paul, 'Christ is formed within you.'

When I am living and walking in the Spirit, the Spirit becomes my starting point for everything. I would not begin to pray without asking the Spirit to be in my words, to turn my words into prayer. Before I switch on the computer, pick up a phone, or ring a doorbell, I whisper a prayer to the Spirit, inviting him to be present in whatever is going to happen. Where the Spirit is more obviously and essentially involved is when I begin a talk, a homily, or am involved in any kind of direction or counselling.

The Spirit is the Great Giver, and his gifts are most precious. In most jobs the person is supplied with a box of tools, or with files for his briefcase. I am staying with a family in the north of Ireland as I write this. The man of the house works for the telephone company. He has a van to travel to his various places of work. He checks a laptop each morning to find out his work assignments for the day. His van contains all the tools he needs to properly do his work, and he has worksheets to record all details of work as they are completed. All of that goes with the job. If he transferred to work with the electricity board, all of that would change. A different van, different tools, and completely different skills.

As a Christian, I am fully equipped with all the 'tools' I need to live the Christian life. In one situation I will need wisdom, discernment, and knowledge, and in another I will need faith, healing, or anointed speaking. The wonderful truth is this: I will *never* be in a situation where there won't be a gift of the Spirit to see me through.

I ring a doorbell to inform parents of the suicide of a son. In human terms, I would dread this moment, not sure what to say to help the situation. When I involve the Spirit in the process, the words I use are totally unimportant; rather it is the Spirit in the words that makes all the difference. Later, when I have left them, I probably won't remember a word I said, but they will, and that's what matters.

I am writing a letter of sympathy to someone on the death of a loved one. I can chew at my pen for hours, writing and rewriting each sentence, always searching for a new and better way of saying something. I am composing the letter, and the letter is from me, and by the time the recipient has read it, the words will have faded into oblivion. On the other hand, I can take a deep breath, call on the Spirit, and just write from the heart. I post the letter without even rereading it. For years to come, the recipient will retain that letter, and will constantly refer to how much it helped at that particular time. (The funny thing is that, by that time, I myself will have completely forgotten a word that I wrote!)

I occasionally have someone come into my office in a very distraught condition. Like a doctor, I open my medicine bag, and find the very treatment that is needed in this particular case. I could speak to the person in such a way that he tells his family when he goes home that I was able to read his mind. (When he has gone out my door, I may not even remember his name!) The wisdom, discernment, knowledge, etc., are available right there for that particular person.

It is important to remember that the gifts are not mine, and they are only available when needed in a particular situation. The gifts are provided for the sake of the other person to whom I minister. Some of the gifts, of course, are for my own private use, like the gift of prayer, or the gift of leadership. To be filled with the Spirit is to be filled with the gifts of the Spirit.

It is important to make a clear distinction between the gifts of the Spirit and the fruits of the Spirit. The gifts come down upon me like tongues of fire. It is like the vertical beam of the cross. When I begin to exercise them in the service of others, this produces the fruits of the Spirit, which is like the horizontal beam of the cross. The fruits are charity, joy, peace, patience, etc. If the gifts do not lead to producing the fruits, then I am like the tree in the gospel story, which had beautiful green foliage but had no fruit. Jesus cursed the tree, and it withered. 'By their fruits you will know them,' says Jesus. The gifts are often used in private, as in praying with the sick, but the fruits always give public witness to the presence of the Spirit. 'A good tree produces good fruit,' Jesus tells us.

Before Jesus ascended into heaven, he had one very important word to leave with his apostles. 'Very soon now you will receive power from on high, and you will be my witnesses onto the ends of the earth.' Notice the two parts of this statement. You will receive, and then you will have to give. I cannot accept the privilege without accepting the responsibility that goes with that privilege. Through the gifts that lead to the fruits, Jesus was preparing his apostles to begin their mission.

Preaching the gospel is a way of living. St Francis of Assisi says that we should always preach the gospel and, only when we have to, we should use words. You are the only gospel that some people may ever read. They may never buy the book. 'You write a new page of the gospel each day, through the things that you do, and the words that you say. People read what you write, whether faithful or true. What is the gospel according to you?' It is very important to get the balance right between the vertical and the horizontal. Jesus bonded both of these beams through his blood, where the divine and the human are sealed as one. What comes down must go sideways, if we are to continue receiving.

The more forgiveness I give to others, the more forgiveness is poured out upon me. I cannot say to God, 'I love you. Thank you. Praise you. I'm sorry,' unless those around me hear that first. 'Whatever you do to the least of my brothers that's what you do onto me.' Just as the Spirit is poured out upon me, so must that Spirit pour out from me into the hearts and the lives of others. Once I receive that outpouring of the Spirit, nothing in my life will ever be the same again. Christianity is about attracting, not about promoting. Whatever it is I have, if it is genuine, others will surely want it. I become a leaven in the community, a presence for good wherever I go.

I headed this chapter *Living and Walking*. Like the crow in a previous story who got the voice-box of a blackbird, I have to practise living and walking in the Spirit. When I was born I had the gift of speech, and the ability to walk, but it took quite a deal of practice and constant endeavour before I could walk or talk freely. The great thing is that I *have* the Spirit, and I am absolutely certain that I will learn to grow in living the life of the Spirit. We are speaking of pure spirituality here, and this must never be confused with religion. Religion is what we do, and spirituality is what the Spirit does. The whole secret is allowing ourselves to be led by the Spirit, and I will speak about that in the following chapter.

Transformation

Living and walking in the Spirit is called the New Life. It is about being born again, and beginning life as completely transformed creatures. The cocoon is broken, the caterpillar is transformed, and a beautiful butterfly lands on your hand.

There is a story that is often used in talks about death, but it also fits in here. There were grubs in the bottom of a bond. Occasionally, one of them felt itself drawn to the surface. The others were wondering what happened when one went up there. They agreed among themselves that the next one called to the surface would return and tell the others what it was like up there. Eventually, one grub made its way towards the surface. He was amazed to find it so bright and so warm up there, with a brilliant light that touched the soul. Suddenly the grub began to change. His whole body went through some sort of transformation that seemed to go on for ages. Eventually, he discovered, to his amazement, that he had become a really beautiful dragonfly. (This was what he was created to be, but he thought that he had settled for always being a grub!) He flew back and forth across the bond. He could see the others below, but they couldn't see him. He then realised that he could not get back. After a while, he gave up any intention of trying to get back, because, he thought, 'They would never recognise a beautiful creature like me as ever being one of them.' A bit far-fetched, I know, but it does point to a very real and deep transformation within, even if I still look like the photo on my passport.

I have known a few people who have had heart transplants. Before the actual operation, they have to go through a long and tedious process. There are x-rays, scans, and every possible way of examining the heart, to determine the amount of damage done, and to decide that it is beyond repair, and needs to be replaced. All of this is explained in great detail to the patient and the next-of-kin. They are shown diagrams of hearts, and they are

shown how the heart will be removed, and the new one trans-
planted. The patient and family are given every option, before
the final decision is made. Eventually, the papers are signed,
and the process is ready to begin. Now the wait begins, as they
wait for a suitable heart. This may happen sooner rather than
later and, indeed, it very well might be too late. Somebody else
has to die, if this man has any hope of living. That person might
already have a donor card, or the next-of-kin could decide that
organs should be donated. The big day comes, and the man sub-
mits himself entirely to others, literally putting his life in their
hands. When we have got to this stage, one very important thing
must happen. The man must be totally removed from the equation. He is given a deep anaesthetic, and he is out of all decision-
making and action for the rest of the operation. Without removing him from the equation, there could be no operation. This is
something that he cannot do for himself, and there is no doubt in
his mind, or in anybody else's, about that fact. I have teased
heart recipients on occasions, asking the spouse if he is more
kind-hearted, more tender-hearted than before. Needless to say
what the answer is, although some people, having had such a
close brush with their mortality, can become much more consid-
erate, grateful, and patient.

To walk again after a heart transplant is to be given a second
chance at life. That is what Pentecost means for us, except that
this second chance is so much more wonderful than the first one.
It is as if the umbilical cord with God is reconnected, and I know
that I am on my way back to the Garden. When the wise men
visited Jesus in Bethlehem, we are told that 'They returned home
by a different route.' Once they had met Jesus they owed nothing to the Herods of this world.

Living the life of the Spirit is like riding the wind like a seagull. The seagull makes the wind do the work, and it can really
have a ball in the midst of the fiercest gales. I once saw a seagull
travel about a mile, turn around, and go back the same way,
without moving a wing. The Spirit is 'the wind beneath my
wings'. The only real sin I can commit, as a Christian, is not to

have hope. 'Always have an explanation to give to those who ask you the reason for the hope that you have,' St Peter tells us. I have a new and eternal hope, and the Spirit has refocused my vision in such a way that I can see the Lord at work in my life. 'Two men looked through their prison bars. One saw the dirt on the street, the other saw the glory of the stars.'

Remembering Peter's story up to, and including Calvary, it makes riveting reading to read his letters. When Jesus returned to Nazareth, the people asked 'Where did this man get this wisdom? He is one of us, and we know his family, and he has grown up among us.' One could ask the same thing about Peter, except that we know what happened to him. The transformation that took place in him on Pentecost morning was most extraordinary. For someone who was afraid of a servant girl some weeks previously, he bounded out of that Upper Room, and with voice raised, he held his listeners spellbound for quite some time. His words were so powerful that thousands of hearts were touched, and many came to believe in the message that he gave. He took the cripple by the hand at the gate of the city, and told him to take up his mat and go home. He looked his accusers in the eye, as he was brought before the Sanhedrin, and he went out and continued the very thing they ordered him not to do. Peter may have looked the way he always looked, and those who knew him could still recognise him. But something within him had changed dramatically, and, in that way, he was a completely different person. The body is not me. I am living in the body. No matter what age the body may be, the child within never grows old. Yes, Peter had changed, changed utterly.

When I was in my mother's womb, being formed in human fashion, I could not understand my mother, or have any ideas whatever about her. When I was born, separated from her, I eventually came to know her face, to recognise her touch, and to respond to her voice. At an earlier stage in my life I was told that I looked like my mother. (With receding hair-line, and expanding waist-line, I am now told 'You're getting more like your father every day'!) I am now in the womb of God, being formed in the image of Jesus Christ. This is the on-going work of the Spirit, that continues quietly but consistently 'until Christ be formed in you'. When we open our hearts to his Spirit, God is free to do in us exactly what he did in Mary. At my first Mass some years ago, I had a song that was sung twice in the Mass, and was printed twice in the handout. 'Be brave little mother for the burden you bear, for it's Christ that you carry everywhere everywhere.' In visiting Elizabeth, Mary did exactly what I would hope to do as a priest, i.e. bring Jesus to someone else.

I have a car outside the door. It means a lot to me because I'm on the road a lot. Supposing the car was stolen, and the culprit was brought into my presence, how do I think I would react? I don't know, actually, but I'm a pacifist by nature, so I hope there would be no violence. Anyhow, to apply this to God, let us look at what he did after the rebellion in the Garden. Human beings wanted to have the power of God. What did God do? If it was his car that was stolen, he forgave the culprit, gave him the car, and provided enough petrol for the rest of his life! He forgave them, and put into operation a plan of salvation that would en-able them share in the fullness of his life, and he provided the Holy Spirit that would enable them live with his life. Only God would do a thing like that.

There are words that must be written bold and clear across the sky, and I must never forget them 'There is nothing impossi-ble for God'. I must never ever set limits to what God can do in me, and certainly wants to do in me. Mary believed that, and the Spirit had complete freedom to work in her. Just as Jesus was 'led by the Spirit' into the desert or down to the Temple, so Mary was ready and willing to be led by the Spirit, no matter where that was. She said her 'yes' on the road to Egypt and on the road to Calvary.

Summarising the last seven chapters, they provide a path to transformation. It is to enter into the fullness of the gospel, and of the life in the Spirit. It is a gift that is available to anyone who wants it. As Peter said on Pentecost morning, 'It is for you and all of your children.' It is to enter into a life that is such that all I will need is the vision to complete it in heaven. There is nothing I will get when I die that I'm not offered now. The road to heaven is itself heaven. An end to guilt, to fear, to emptiness, and to religion. It is to enter into 'the freedom of the children of God' as St Irenaus put it. While enjoying the gift of life, and being truly grateful for it, it also engenders a sort of divine home-sickness for my True Home. It is not possible for me to be grateful and unhappy at the same time.

Because of the process outlined in the last seven chapters, as someone with a Senior Citizen's free pass, I have never been as grateful in my life, and I have never been happier than I am now. I can only hope that what I have written may help someone else to discover this pearl of great price.

Out of the boat

In an earlier chapter I spoke about having to step out of the boat if you want to walk on water. Nothing ventured, nothing gained. I grow in faith by practice, and that journey consists of constant decisions and regular usage.

I like St Peter. Oh, he was brash, and sometimes not too cautious, but over-caution will be the death of us all. 'Lord, if you want to, you can bid me come to you on the water.' Who but Peter would have suggested it? He had a big heart, and oodles of goodwill, even though he was really a kitten within. Jesus loved Peter because he dared to venture. He didn't do too well when the pressure came on him but, at least, he wanted to be there with Jesus, and for him, as best he could. He grabbed the sword in the garden, because that was the only way he knew how to defend. He took the risk of following John into the courtyard where Jesus was a prisoner. The fact that he panicked and lost his nerve is something that Jesus could easily understand, and forgive. Later on, when he had 'fished all night and caught nothing', at Jesus' word he was willing to give it another go. Very few of us are asked to be in the front line like Peter, but we all get many opportunities to step out in faith.

The centurion must have been an extraordinary man. He was a Roman and a pagan, yet he dared to break ranks and go 'to the enemy' to look for help, no matter what anybody else thought of him. No wonder Jesus was impressed by him, and declared that he 'had not found faith like this in Israel'.

The springboard for jumping out of the boat, for letting go of our fears and insecurities, is a very clear conviction of helplessess and powerlessess, and the acceptance that we just have to go elsewhere to get the help we want. There is a direct connection between the depth and scope of our faith, and our own sense of inadequacy. If we think that there's the slightest chance that we might be able to manage this on our own, we will hold back from looking elsewhere. When many of his listeners turned and walked away, Jesus asked the apostles, 'Will you also walk away?' Once again it was Peter to the fore with a resounding response, 'Lord, where else can we go? You alone have the words of eternal life. We know, and we believe that you are the Christ, the Son of the Living God.'

There is one scene in the gospels that impresses me more than most. Jesus was in the house of a Pharisee, and many other Pharisees had joined him there. As usual, they were keeping a watching brief, lest he say or do something that they might use against him. Into that very house came a woman who 'had a bad name in the town'. Boy, did she take a risk! She walked straight into the lion's den. The woman was desperate. She was guilty, afraid, lonely, and very unloved. She knew there was only one place she could go, only one person she could approach. With extraordinary courage and faith, she walked right into that house, and went straight to Jesus. Despite the stares, the sneers, and the sense of shock that surrounded her, she knew that she had found a safe place. She actually risked her very life by walking into that house, because she might easily have been dragged out and stoned to death. Talking about stepping over the side of the boat! In the full glare of animosity and hostility, she interrupted whatever was going on, and she threw herself at the feet of Jesus. She began to cry, and she let her tears fall on the feet of Jesus, as she began to wash the dust of the roads from them. By now her whole attention was on Jesus, and she was past caring what the onlookers might think. She washed his feet, and proceeded to dry them with her hair. Her tears were the only water she had, and her hair the only towel. She did all she could with the little she had. Then she produced a jar of precious ointment, and began to anoint the feet of Jesus.

Meanwhile, Jesus was very conscious of those who looked on, and he knew exactly what they were thinking. 'If this man were a prophet he would surely know what kind of woman this is,' they muttered. Jesus spoke. He did not have to directly defend the woman or plead for understanding of her situation. He pointed out to the owner of the house some of the services that he had neglected, services that were normally accorded important visitors who came from some distance. The Pharisee had not offered facilities for Jesus to wash and dry his feet, but this woman made use of what little she had to provide him with that service. The woman now produced a box of precious ointment, and proceeded to anoint the feet of Jesus, so that the perfume filled the whole room they were in. This really was pushing the Pharisees to the limits. Jesus delivered his greatest salvo when he announced that this public sinner had her sins forgiven 'because she has loved much'.

If sin is alienation from God, how could this woman do what she did for Jesus and be alienated from God at the same time? The woman took the risk, she dared to do what she felt she had to do, and she won God's favour and approval. Jesus went further when he declared that 'wherever the gospel is preached, what this woman has done will be spoken of'. She is one of the many people I am looking forward to meeting in heaven.

When Jesus tells us that the Holy Spirit will never leave us, he is saying that he will never lead us where his Spirit will not be there to see us through. If I have a cardiac unit, a wheelchair, or a cancer ward waiting for me down the road, I will get all that I need to be at peace there, and to deal with that situation. 'I will never leave you, or abandon you in the storm.' Even if life leads you to Egypt or to Calvary, you can be sure that his Spirit will be with you in every moment and movement of that journey. You need have no worry what the future holds, if you believe that he holds the future.

When I speak about stepping out of the boat, I am not thinking of acting irresponsibly, without common prudence or caution. I am speaking about those decisions we have to make, and those situations we have to face that can have us frozen into inactivity, afraid to move one way or another. I am speaking of those times when I put my hand in the hand of the Lord, and I 'go for it'. The fact that I don't know the outcome is where faith comes in. If I knew the result I wouldn't need faith. The Lord didn't let Peter drown, no more than he will abandon you when you step out in faith. Many a time I have found myself facing situations where I had every reason to be conscious of my inadequacies.

I was asked to give a Retreat to the bishops and priests of the United Arab Emirates. I said 'yes', knowing they were multi-lingual, and the job seemed impossible. When the Abbot of a Cistercian Monastery asked me last year to give a six-day Retreat to the community, I said 'yes', and only then did I begin to think of what on earth I'd speak about for six days! The way I figure this is that, when someone, like the Abbot, asked me to do something, it was the Lord's way of telling me that I would have what it takes when the time comes. The gift would not be given to me, but to the community, through the message I would deliver.

With each call comes the grace to respond to that call. I will never come to believe this until I practise it again and again. My faith can grow like the grain of mustard seed, which is the smallest of all seeds. I remember looking at mustard trees in the garden of Gethsemane, and then requiring a strip of cello tape to pick up mustard seeds, because I could not grip them with my fingers. Jesus says that the birds of the air will come and find shelter in those trees. In other words, people of faith often find that others come to them for prayers when they're in trouble, and their faith provides a source of shelter for the troubled one. An enclosed community of Sisters are usually inundated with requests for prayers from people near and far. The community is like one of those mustard trees that Jesus spoke of.

I spoke earlier of the woman who washed and dried the feet of Jesus, and how I looked forward to meeting her in heaven. There is another little woman whom I would love to meet, and that is the one who reached out and touched the hem of Jesus' garment. I don't know how long she thought about this, or how many times she nearly did it, but held back. My own suspicion is that this is the first time she got near enough to Jesus to be able to do what her heart told her to do. She felt she was taking a great risk, and when Jesus asked who touched him, she was sure she was in serious trouble. What an extraordinary little woman she was! I say 'little', because independent of her stature, she was obviously a very humble little woman. It is very clear what drove her to such a simple act of faith and bravery. She was desperate, and she had no doubt that her healing was not to be found elsewhere. Like the rest of us she had tried everything else, and, like us, she found that nothing had worked for her. She saw in Jesus a new hope. She saw something that touched her spirit, and, risk or no risk, she just could not let the moment of grace pass.

When Bartimeus, the blind man, who sat on the side of the road, heard that 'Jesus of Nazareth was passing by', he had just a moment in which to make a decision. He could let Jesus pass on down the road, and die a blind man, or he could grab the opportunity with both hands, and be free of his ailment.

These are moments of grace that come our way on a regular basis. We can grab them or let them pass. To grab them is to step out, if not out of the boat, at least in some form of reaching out. As far as Bartimeus was concerned, Jesus would have kept going, and would have passed him by, had not Bartimeus chosen to stop him. The more he shouted, the more the crowds told him to be quiet. But there was no stopping him. He knew what he wanted, and he knew where he'd get it. 'I once was blind, but now I see.'

It is sad to think that I could live my life and never really experience the power of God, all because I was afraid to take a risk. Jesus gives us 147 promises in the gospels, and there is not one might or one maybe in the whole lot. Elizabeth praised Mary, because 'You believed that the promises of the Lord would be fulfilled.' 'The sin of this world is unbelief in me,' says Jesus. Prudence and caution can stultify us into inaction, and we end up having settled for existing rather than living. 'I came that you should have life, and have it in abundance.' Jesus speaks of a life of abundance, and the only limits to that abundance are the ones I set. What a pity!

Letting go

As recently as last week I had a spin in an ambulance to the local hospital. I have had several such trips over the past few years but, thankfully, the good Lord has something left for me to do. About three years ago I was taken to hospital on a Saturday night. All day Sunday and Monday, as I lay there, looking like a spaceman, with oxygen mask, two drips coming into me, and one tube coming out of me, I quietly concluded that 'This is it!' (I found out later that week that the doctor thought the same!) Anyhow, my abiding memory was the peace I experienced, and my willingness to say 'yes' to whatever the Lord wanted for me.

I knew then that I did not have the Brownie points, the Green Shield stamps, the merits, indulgences, and graces that I had set out many years ago, to collect for such an emergency! All of those mattered little anymore, because I was sure that all would be well. I had no idea before that what it would feel like to be in that situation. (I heard of a man who said he wouldn't mind dying when he was ninety, and that was grand until he reached 89!) My abiding memory of that time was my complete willing-ness to let go. I would never have rated myself very high on the 'letting go' stakes during my lifetime, but now, somehow, it was different. I was quite resigned, and my over-riding emotion was one of gratitude for family, for friends, and for my work as a priest, something through which I have been enormously blessed.

Self-preservation is the number one basic instinct, and it has to be said that nobody likes the thought of death. However, when it seemed to come knocking on my door, I found a ready willingness to let go, and put my faith and trust in the mercy and love of God. That experience of being willing to let go has had a profound effect on my life ever since. If I was willing to let go of life, how much easier is it to let go of resentments, of regrets, or of possessions. I have thought long and deep about this, and I find that the idea of 'letting go' is figuring more and more in my list of priorities. I am not at all surprised that the concept should get a chapter in this collection of insights.

It is absolutely vital to let go of the past, because the past no longer exists, and what's the point of holding on to something that doesn't exist anymore? The only value the past has are the lessons it taught me. I would be a very wise person today if I learned every lesson that life taught me.

Jesus told us 'You are my friends'. There is an Arabian definition of a friend that I like. 'A friend is somebody to whom one can pour out all the contents of one's heart, wheat and chaff together, knowing that gentle hands will sift it, keep what is worth keeping and, with the breath of love, will blow the chaff away.' That's what Jesus does with my past. He garners the nuggets of wisdom that life has taught, and entrusts them to me as something precious that must never be forgotten, and he blows the rest away.

Many people remain imprisoned in their past, and they live on a constant diet of guilt, remorse, and hindsight, with overlayers of bitterness, hurts, and unforgiveness that stifle any hope of living today with any kind of peace or happiness. Jesus is there as Saviour, with both hands held out, ready and willing to take all of that from me, if I will just allow him.

When Jesus asks me 'Who do you say that I am?', I have to give serious thought to my answer. If I am imprisoned in the past, then he is not my Saviour. We say 'By your cross and resurrection you have set us free', but I may not be free at all.

When I was growing up in the country all those years ago, there was a man who used come around buying hens. He would tie the legs of the hen and throw her into the cart with all the others. One day he gave us local yokels a simple lesson in hen psychology. He reached in with a pen-knife and snipped the twine tying the legs of one of the hens. She didn't move, even though I expected her to fly away. He explained that hens are stupid in that, if the others are not free, that hen will have no idea that she's free! If he snipped the twine tying all the legs they would all fly away. If I live among people who are trapped in the past, I may well pick up their dis-ease. A great deal of our sectarian strife is a direct result of what happened in the past.

The sins of the fathers are visited on their children. There would never be a war if somebody somewhere was prepared and ready to say 'I'm sorry. I was wrong.' When everybody is right, then the truth goes out the window, and injustice reigns supreme. Each of our World Wars was supposed to 'end all wars'. Today we see Vietnam being repeated in Iraq, and the carnage continues. The future is being jeopardised because of something that happened in the past, because of something that cannot be undone. The past has not taught the wisdom to ensure that such things might be avoided in the future. 'Lord, give me the serenity to accept the things I cannot change; courage to change the things I can, and the wisdom to know the difference.'

Sometimes we have to let go of our dreams, if we are to live in the real world. Mary dreams of marrying some wealthy hand-some hulk, and she ends up married to Joe Bloggs, who could hardly light a fire, not to speak of setting the world on fire. If Mary holds on to her dream, she's not going to be too happy with poor Joe! I remember meeting a young mother in New York who was striving her utmost to rear her children just as her mother had reared her in a very rural part of Ireland. If she is ever to live in reality, then she will have to let go of the dream. She is functioning at one level, but thinking at another level. That can never bring happiness. To look around me, seeing everyone and everything there, and to be willing to say 'yes' to that, is to bloom where I'm planted.

I am not implying that, if what I see is very wrong, I should resign myself to that. I am speaking of the situation where life is normal, and as good as could be expected. Traditionally, it has been the dream of every Jew to return to live in the Promised Land, and many of them have done that over the years. The story is told of one man standing praying at the Wailing Wall, praying over and over again 'I want to be with my people. I want to be with my people.' Someone near him whispered

'Aren't you with your people here? Where are your people?' 'In Miami in Florida,' came the reply!

Alcoholics are noted for what is called 'doing a geographic'. If I could only get to Australia, and start again, I would cut out the drink entirely. Needless to say, give him enough time in Australia, and he will discover that he brought his problem with him.

'Let go, and let God' is a phrase with which we are all familiar. It is a very simple way of saying that we should stop playing God. God will become God in my life the very second I decide to stop playing God. God will not gate-crash my party if he is not invited.

It can be difficult to really understand what is meant when we speak about handing something over to God. I remember a young mother, many years ago, whose husband died of cancer, and she was left with three young boys. The third one was the one who seemed to give her the most trouble. When I suggested that she hand him over to God, she threw her hands in the air, and said, 'I hand him over to God every morning, but God gives him back to me by ten o'clock!' Handing my will and my life over to the care of God is something that is worth trying to grasp as a way of doing things.

There is a very simple test to know if you are doing God's will. Would God approve how you treated that person this morning? Would God approve how you spend your time or your money? If you believe that he would, then you are doing his will. It's as simple as that. It can become a way of measuring the quality of our lives, and I will often have to give up my own will, and let go of my own selfishness, if I am to act in a way with which God is pleased.

If I am on my way back to the Garden where an eternal hug awaits me, then I have to become a hugger on the way, as my forgiveness extends wider and wider until there is no one left to forgive. This can take quite a lot of letting go. Some people bury the hatchet, but they mark the spot, in case they ever need it again! It is not very realistic to speak about *forgiving and forgetting*.

Some people have been hurt in ways which they could never possibly forget. The pain of remembering begins to ease, though, once the forgiving process gets under way. It is possible, and is quite frequently the case, where the forgiveness is given, but the memory is as vivid as ever. I cannot hurry up the forgetting process; that will take time. Even the forgiving will need time. I have to start with a desire to forgive, even if I am not yet ready to do so. I don't believe the Lord would put that desire in my heart without giving me what it takes to carry it through. When I forgive, I set myself free. When I have a resentment against another, it is as if I were drinking poison and expecting the other person to die! Unforgiveness is a self-inflicted prison, where I sit in solitary confinement, licking my wounds, and counting my hurts.

The word 'resentment' comes from the French 'sentir', or the Latin 'sentare', both of which mean 'to feel'. To re-sent is to feel all over again. In other words, I continue to put myself through the pain and, as a result, the anger and need for revenge grows within me. I could walk right out into freedom by letting go, and pressing the erase button. This is an area where letting go is of paramount importance.

At the beginning of this chapter I spoke about the letting go that is involved in dying. That is one letting go that I cannot escape. I would suggest that I have many opportunities every single day to practise that letting go in many other areas, and that will make the final letting go all that much easier. Death is like a pile of sand at the end of my life, which I can take and sprinkle along the road of life, as I die to myself in so many different ways, i.e. my tiredness, possessions, opinions etc. If I do this dying during my life I will find that there's no sand left when I get to the end, and I'll be all set for my ascension, with nothing to hold me down. On the other hand, if I wait till the end of my life to die, it very well could be too late ...

On all cylinders

Everybody dies, but not everybody lives. Some people settle for existing and, when they die, you will need a doctor to certify that, because there hasn't been much life there at any time. You could write on their tomb-stones 'Died at forty, buried at eighty'! I'm not worried about life after death, but it does concern me about how much life there is before death. I would much prefer to burn out than rust out. I get one shot at life, and I should give it all I've got. 'I shall pass this way but once. Any good deed that I can do, any good word that I can say, let me do it now, let me say it now, for I shall never pass this way again.' Each and every birthday comes only once, as the sands of time continue to flow, and no one can put a stop to the march of time.

Life consists of many journeys. We travel from dependence to independence, to interdependence. Believe it or not, even if often said as a joke, life does begin at forty! Up till that time, the average person is 'building': building a home, a family, a profession, a niche in society, etc. Under normal circumstances, the pressure should be off by forty, and the person should be free to give back something to life. If life continues to be high-pressured, either the demands of the job are too much, or the person is over-ambitious to achieve. Stopping to smell the flowers would not be on, because time has become money, and some people can never get enough of that. Some people know the price of everything, and the value of nothing. Life is a mystery to be lived, not a problem to be solved. For some people, however, it is a relentless battle to be waged, a competition that must be won, and a process of self-aggrandisement that is endless. The end sometimes arrives as a heart attack on a golf course in their mid-forties.

Jesus came that we should have life, and have it to the full. He speaks about life in abundance. God wants us to enjoy his precious gift of life. He gives me nothing for myself. He doesn't give me my gift of speech to go around talking to myself! Life is something to be given away, to be invested for the good of others, and the reward of such a life is a life of eternal happiness with God and with all those whose lives have enriched the lives of others.

I remember processing with about eighty-thousand others towards the Heyshal Stadium in Brussels. The King and Queen of Belgium were there, as was Cardinals Suenens and Daniels. We were celebrating the centenary of the birth of Blessed Damien, the 'leper priest', who spent a mere fifteen years of his life in one of the remotest islands in the Pacific, ministering to lepers. It was a national holiday in Belgium, and all of the country had come to a stand-still for the occasion. Every branch of government, military, church, and industry was involved in the celebration. As I returned from that Stadium, I was thinking that that was also the centenary of the birth of Hitler, and most of the world didn't even know that. *Sic transit gloriam mundi!* ('Thus passes the glory of the world.')

The earlier part of our lives usually has to do with education. The word 'education' comes from the Latin word '*educare*', which, literally means 'to lead out'. If you do not have the gift of music, you can go for piano lessons for the rest of your life, and you may not get past the one-finger playing of notes. The education process is to discover what gifts you already have, and to bring those out. Unfortunately, very few of my generation experienced this, as we were all corralled into maths, languages, science, geography, etc, some of which were completely beyond us, because you cannot put in a gift, and you cannot develop a gift that is not there in the first place. Very few people ever become completely educated, in so far as it is reckoned that the average person lives a life, and discovers about 25% of the gifts they've got. I do not have a gift for music, for art, or for technology. I discovered one gift I had, i.e. the gift of communication, and, through talks, books, tapes, videos, radio, and television, I have developed that gift to a fairly satisfactory degree. I do not regret the lack of other gifts, but I sometimes wonder if there is a talent or two there that will never be discovered. Grandma Moses was an old lady in a retirement home. To exercise her arthritic fingers, a member of staff gave her a set of paints and brushes. Straightaway she began to produce masterpieces and, if you wanted one of her paintings today, you would have to be in the millionaire bracket to put in an offer.

I wouldn't be too uptight about the possible waste of talent, because none of us is going to discover the full package anyhow. I'll offer one example that does bother me. God gives us gifts, and he tells us what those gifts are by sending people to us, asking for assistance in a particular area. Obviously, the other person believes that I have what it takes to be of help in that situation. The problem begins when I come to discover my own talents! I have been giving Retreats for years, because I am always been called on to do that. I am writing this book in response to endless requests from friends that I put this material on paper. The guy who discovers his own gifts is the one who stands up at the party and insists on singing a song, even though he is the only one in that room who believes he can sing! On the other hand, there is someone else in that room, and everybody is calling on him or her to sing. That request must be taken seriously, and any sort of 'Ah, I can't sing; I don't know the words of any song, etc,' should be seen as the untruth that it is, and the person can be seen as someone who doesn't appreciate a gift that God has given them for the sake of others. I hate having to 'coax' and humour someone into singing, playing the piano, etc. I would ask them once, and if they don't respond, I would look for someone else.

Jesus tells two stories of people who were entrusted with talents, and who were later called up to give an account of how they used and invested those talents. The greatest thanks I could give God for having a good voice, is to make it available, when asked, to those who want to enjoy it. To continue with the gift of voice for a moment, this can become a wonderful and very blessed form of ministry, when used at weddings, funerals, etc. I have heard songs at funerals that were most consoling, and songs at weddings that were uplifting and inspiring. The word 'artist' covers quite a broad field. They are in the business of creation; of taking the orderly and mundane, and transforming it into a thing of beauty and a joy forever. How bereft our world would be today without our painters, sculptors, and designers. They have the ability to see what the non-artist cannot see, and they have the ability to translate that into reality. Some painting and sculptures have had a riveting effect on me, and they opened my soul to a beauty I had forgotten. These artists make a wonderful contribution to our world, and the world is much richer because they lived, and gave of what they had.

Life is fragile, handle with prayer. Life is not manageable. One heart attack, and it's all over. I own nothing. Everything I have is on loan, and God can claim it back whenever he thinks it is the right time. One of the ways in which I can get some grip on life is to break it down into sections of 24 hours. When I woke up this morning I was given a gift. It is a very rare gift that was never before given to a human being, and will never again be given to anybody. It is the 25th day of January 2007. Because it is a gift, maybe that's why we call it the present. Written on the book are the words 'batteries included'. With each day comes whatever I will need to live that day. Jesus calls it 'our daily bread'. There is nothing that will happen today that the good Lord and myself won't be able to deal with. That goes for each day, with their many varieties of problems. One of those days will be my last and, on that day, I will also get what it will take to go through the process of dying and death.

To live life to the full I must consciously accept the gift of each new day. I need to develop a constant sense of gratitude for each day as it comes. A pop star was interviewed on television recently, and among the questions asked was, 'Tell me some-thing for which you are really grateful.' His answer came as a surprise. 'I am grateful that I woke up this morning.' Each day has its own graces, its own opportunities, and requires its own 'yes' to life. A good life is a collection of days well lived. When you were born, you alone cried, and everybody else was very happy. You should live your life in such a way that, when you die, you will be very happy and everybody else will be crying! (Mark Twain said that we should live our lives in such a way that, when we die, even the undertaker will be sorry!)

I have a choice. I can waken up in the morning with a growl 'Good God, morning!', or with a prayer 'Good morning, God!' My daily bread is measured to my needs. I may be confined to bed, I may be quite limited in my mobility, or I may have quite demanding responsibilities in the course of this day. If I take this day as a mini-life, and try to keep things within the day, it may be much easier than I expected. If, of course, I am back in the past with guilt, or off in the future with worry, then today will be a real burden indeed. By keeping life within the day, I am dealing with manageable portions of my life, and not trying to resolve everything in one day.

All I can do is do my best, and that is all that can be expected. Life is not something that happens to me, as if I were some sort of powerless robot, with no say in how things are. Hilary Pole was a physical education instructress in Birmingham some years ago. At age 27 she developed a rare muscular disease that completely immobilised her. The only movement she had in her whole body was a sixteenth of an inch with her big toe. A Cambridge professor devised a sort of Morse code typewriter on which she began to practise. She wrote poetry, and all of her poems were about the joy of living. She received an OBE from the Queen for her endeavours. One of her poems includes the following lines. 'You ask me if I'm sad or bored, or if my life it is abhorred. And I tell I am not; that I can now accept my lot. I remind your sadly shaking head, it's my body, not my mind, in bed.' I cried because I had no shoes until I saw a man who had no feet. Never stop thanking God for the gift of life, for the gift of today, and for the gift of now …

Living and laughing

George Burns, the comedian, lived to be a hundred, and it was wonderful that he was given such a gift, because he lived and laughed his way out to the very end. Towards the end of his life he said that, every morning when he woke up, the first thing he did was check the death column in the paper and, if his name wasn't there, he got up! On his ninetieth birthday he said that the great thing about being ninety is that you know everything, and the big disadvantage is that you cannot remember any of it. On his hundredth birthday he said, 'When I was a young man, I used get a standing ovation, and now, at 100, I get an ovation for standing!' A year before his hundredth birthday he announced that, on that day he was going to hire Caesar's Palace in Las Vegas, and give a whooping big party for all his friends ... 'That is, if Caesar's Palace is still there!'

Laughter is a wonderful tonic, and it is not possible to laugh and have a nervous breakdown at the same time! A kid asked in school one time if God had a sense of humour, and I replied, 'Does he what? You'd want to come and see some of the people he created. He has got to have an extraordinary sense of humour!' It is a mistake to take life, or ourselves, too seriously. We'll be dead long enough.

I believe that Jesus had a wonderful roguish sense of humour. When the woman at the well was holding forth about where people should worship, and what was right, and what was wrong, he whispered out of the corner of his mouth, 'Go home and get your husband!' Now the woman had a problem because she was now with husband number seven, and Jesus knew only too well. However, it was one way of stopping her gallop!

Peter held no surprises for Jesus. Bold and brash, but with a heart of gold, Jesus loved Peter, and he poked light fun out of him whenever he got a chance. When Peter boldly volunteered

to step over the side of the boat and walk on water, Jesus, con-
cealing a smile, just said, 'Come on'. Jesus was ready for the inevitable and, of course, when Peter lost his nerve and began to
sink, Jesus was right there, with his hand stretched out to hold
him up. Before Good Friday, Peter had boasted that, no matter
what any of the others did, he would be there for Jesus through
thick and thin. Of course, once the pressure came, Peter caved
in. After his resurrection, Jesus called Peter aside, and whispered a question, 'Well, Peter, what do you think now? Do you
still love me more than these?' He wasn't poking fun at Peter, he
was just light-heartedly reminding him of what he had said before, and he hoped Peter may have learned a lesson from it.

The scene involving the woman who was about to be stoned
to death is a very powerful story in every way. It clearly illus-
trates, yet again, where Jesus stood when it came to judgement
and condemnation. It also has its humorous side. Jesus knelt
down on the ground, and began to write with his finger in the
sand. We are not told what he was writing, but it may have
made some of the onlookers very uncomfortable. He let them
sweat it out for a while, and then, probably restraining a smile,
he turned to them and calmly suggested that the one among
them who was without sin should throw the first stone. The silence was deafening. The movement was gradual, was very definite. One by one, they began to move and walk away. Not one
of them remained. Jesus must have enjoyed that because, at
least, the truth had prevailed. He was extremely clever, and he
must have had a certain sense of black humour to walk them
into such a trap of their own making.

It is easy to imagine Jesus smiling, and nowadays one finds
the occasional picture that depicts that. Anyone who knows
anything about children, knows only too well that children just
don't go to anyone in the crowd. They detect the warmth, and
they respond to the smile. They gathered around him, and he
put them sitting on his knee. Not every child will allow a complete
stranger do that. It had to be the smile that was infectious and
inviting. It had to be the laugh, and a sense of roguish humour,

because it is normal and natural to play with children. You tickle them, make faces at them, peep through your fingers at them, and make funny sounds with your voice. I honestly believe that Jesus could and did do all these things.

For many people, religion is very serious business. We dress up in our Sunday best, and wear our most pious faces. I often speak of 'the transforming power of holy water'. The people get out of their cars at the church on Sunday morning. They shout across at neighbours, enquire about a sick one, or if there's anyone going to the football match today. Once they put their finger in the holy water font, something happens to them. Their faces become drained of life. All smiles are gone; the frowns return. The eyes are cast down, and they make their way very cautiously towards some corner where they will be least conspicuous. At the sign of peace someone holds out a hand that feels more like a dead fish, and we all look forward again. (One of my colleagues had a bright idea one Sunday morning and, just as a change, he suggested that people should turn to the person behind them with a sign of peace. Imagine the surprise when each person turned around to find that the person behind was looking back at the person behind, and all were looking out the back door! That was one occasion when laughter was acceptable in church!)

Coming out of the church the reverse process occurs. Once those fingers touch that holy water, life returns to that face, the frowns are gone, and the smile returns. Once outside the door they become human (!) again, and resume enquiring about sick folks, and about someone who died during the night. Even when they get into their cars, people can be seen to lower a window and have an animated conversation with someone in the car beside them.

God has blessed me with the grace of having a great love for the Eucharist, and a deep appreciation of the privilege of celebrating Eucharist. Thank God, he also has blessed me with a sense of humour, and there is no way that I can leave that behind me in the sacristy when I go out on the altar! I assure them that I will pay strict attention to what I'm saying this morning, because I've just heard of a bishop who dreamt he was preaching a sermon, and he woke, and he was! The first morning I appeared for Mass as parish priest, I knew that my every move and turn were being watched very closely. When I saw people leaving the church at Communion time, I calmly went over to the mike and said a prayer 'for the faithful departed'. They were afraid to move the next Sunday! I found that a sense of humour was much more effective than a scolding.

I believe that a lot of our 'seriousness' in the area of religion comes from the kind of personal God we worship. If God is to be feared, then you have very little to laugh about, because he'll have the last laugh. If it becomes a question of accumulating graces and indulgences, then it becomes hard work, and there's so much to be done, and maybe so little time left, that we have to make the most of every minute. It is really sad to think that I might not be happy with God, and my thoughts about him are not happy ones. When Jesus speaks of joy, he says, 'My joy will be in you.' We are told that 'Jesus was filled with the joy of the Spirit.' He was ecstatic with joy. He speaks about his joy 'pressed down and flowing over'.

I honestly think it is seriously wrong to take religion too seriously (if you get my point!). Of course, religion is important, because it has to do with God, and our relationship with him. But do you think that God, unlike the priest on the altar, is upset at that child that is crying, or the other climbing over the bench? God looks at the heart, and he wants our hearts to be happy. He wants us to be as relaxed and as normal in his house as we are in our own. I often joke about some of our more serious parishioners, and the problems they might face when they enter the joys and delights of heaven. Because of lack of practice, they may have a problem with the joyful singing, and all the harps, and the clapping of hands!

I occasionally have an experience that gives me great joy. I arrive for a Novena in a parish. In some parishes, some people don't look at me for the first few nights. Their heads are bowed, and they are in deep reflection. Maybe, about the fifth night, we'll begin to get the smiles and, hopefully, before the Novena ends, we will have had a few good laughs. Apart from all religious aspects, I would consider that a success in itself. 'If you are saved, you're supposed to look saved! And if you're happy, tell your face, and then we'll all know it!' If the witness value of Christianity doesn't include a smile, then we're in serious trouble.

Christianity is about attracting, rather than about promoting. You are the message, and it is you who will attract, rather than anything you preach. If I go into your house, and I tell you I have measles, when I actually have chicken-pox, which are you going to catch? The gospel is good news that has often been turned into good advice. There should be dancing in the streets where the gospel is proclaimed.

One Sunday morning, with a dead-pan face, I told the people about what happened the previous night. There was a bus passing the church as the people came out from Saturday evening Mass, and someone remarked 'Ah, there must be a funeral.' 'Now there was no sign of a hearse or a coffin, so it must have been the looks on the faces of the people coming out that gave the idea that it had to be a funeral.' I think they got the point!

'Lighten up a little' is a phrase one sometimes hears. What I'm saying in this chapter is *Lighten up a lot* … Life is a mystery to be lived, not a problem to be solved. Relax those muscles, ungrit those teeth, unclench those fists. Life is for living, and it is also for giving. Brighten up someone else's life, someone else's home. There's so much good to be done that we haven't time for moaning. If heaven begins now, then let's begin the celebrations now. Our vocation is not about getting to heaven. Jesus has taken care of that. Our vocation has everything to do with getting heaven down here. Where there is despair, let me bring your hope; where there is sadness, let me bring your joy. It's much more difficult to get heaven into people than it is to get people into heaven. Go for it … and enjoy it.

Waiting and watching

God waits for us to wait for him. 'All good things come to us in God's own time' is a saying used by an older generation. Waiting is part of being poor. The poor are always waiting; waiting for a break, for a handout, for help of any kind. Beggars can't be choosers, so they have no choice but to wait. The bureaucracy of World Banks and Third World agencies will require more long and tedious meetings, more reports, and further scientific research, while the people of Darfur are dying of hunger, and are absolutely helpless to speed up the process. The refugee woman sits with her back to a wall with her hand held out. She has to wait. Somebody will stop and notice her, but she has to wait for that recognition. The Jewish people are still waiting for their Messiah.

When Simeon took that child in his arms in the Temple, he knew that his waiting was over. This is the day he had longed for; this is the day he probably thought was not going to come in his lifetime. He was ready to die happy, because his waiting was over. All good things come to those who wait.

It requires humility to have the patience to wait. The proud and the arrogant stride to the very top of the queue. They do not ask; they demand. God's gifts are their rights, and probably less than one in ten come back to say thanks. One of the ten lepers was a Samaritan. He had no religion, had never been to the Temple, and he had no expectations of a Messiah. Yet, of all the ten, he was the only one to come back to say thanks. The others probably had done their time at religious services earlier in life, and so God owed them one. The Pharisee wasn't very conscious of God's gifts to him. He was more aware of how God must be so pleased with him for being so perfect in every way. 'Lord, it's so hard to be humble …'

'Watch and pray that you enter not into temptation' were Jesus' words to his apostles as they entered the garden of

Gethsemane. I mustn't forget that Satan is also listening in when I pray. He can head me off at any point.

I remember something that happened when I was a school chaplain some years ago. The Oratory was quite close to my office. I had some free time, so I decided to cross over to the Oratory to spend some quiet time there. As I came out of my office, I noticed something on the notice-board that caught my eye. I began to read it. There were other notices there that I had not read before. I was still reading when the hooter sounded for the end of class, and I had not made it to the Oratory. I had neither watched nor prayed! I fell into that trap on many an occasion, when I had intended spending some quiet time with the Lord, and the phones began to ring, and I remembered dozens of things I had to do and, with hindsight, I saw that none of them was urgent, and could be attended to at some other time. I can get so busy with the urgent that I overlook the important.

It is important to be watchful, to have a watchful disposition. This is part of being prayerful, part of the contemplative dimension of our lives. If I really want to become prayerful, then I'll just have to become watchful. I wear the antennae on my head, and I don't sleep-walk into situations. 'Lead us not into temptation.' God does not lead us into temptation but, what we ask for is that, like a Loving Father, he would watch over us, and prevent us walking into landmines, into situations where we would be too weak to resist the lures of the evil one. Satan is so much cleverer then we are, and, without the overshadowing power of God, we could be led in whatever direction Satan chooses.

The story of the Prodigal Son is one that should always move us. We cannot be untouched by the thought of the father watching and waiting (and hoping) day after day. He spent hours scanning the horizon every day, and it must have been difficult to maintain his hope. Finally, his hopes were fulfilled, as he recognised his son from quite a distance away. Yes, indeed, all good things come to those who wait. The sight of his son made every waiting moment worthwhile. There is a legend in the

Russian Orthodox Church about the day of the General Judgement. The people are joyfully flocking in the gates of heaven. Jesus is standing outside the gate, with his hand shading his eye from the sun, as he stares off into the distance. Somebody asks him what is he doing, and he says, 'I'm waiting for Judas'. It's never too late for God.

Jesus speaks of the kingdom of God in the following manner. 'A man throws seed on the land. Night and day, while he sleeps, when he is awake, the seed is sprouting and growing; how, he does not know. Of its own accord, the land produces first the shoot, then the ear, then the full grain in the ear. And when the crop is ready, he loses no time; he starts to reap because the harvest has come.'

The kingdom of God is built up by tiny acts, and most of them are hidden. There is no way that the process can be speeded up. A lot of our food stuff is lacking in proper nourishment, because it is grown in artificial conditions, and the chemicals have more to do with the growth than the ground in which the seed was sown. *Festina lente* ... make haste slowly.

My favourite food is that which is cooked in a slow cooker, where the meat and vegetables are left cooking all day long at a low temperature. One feels that all the goodness has been extracted and saved, and what is best in that food is put out on the plates. We live in an age when everything is becoming more instant, and the emphasis is on saving time and effort. I'm not complaining about this because, in the normal evolution of life, everything is in a state of flux, a state of constant change. However, I do want to salvage the most precious things: those things that require time, waiting, and great patience, if the proper result is to be achieved.

This has to do with the spiritual, but it also has to do with serious dimensions of the physical as well. Relationships take time to grow maturely, because it takes a long time to really know another person. 'Whirlwind romances' are all very well, and I am always glad when they prove successful, but it can be a dangerous game. Having the ability to wait and to watch is a disposition, and is a chief characteristic of wisdom. Maturity is to be in charge, to be in control, so situations and circumstances do not make my decisions for me. If I have any dimension of God in my life, then I have to learn to wait, because it is in the waiting that my faith and my hope can grow, and become strong.

The long years of training required for many professions must be very off-putting for those who don't understand. Of course, I could learn all the theory in quarter that time, but the process involves much than just theories. The information leads to formation, and that cannot be short-circuited in any way. The young mother hopes and prays that her baby will complete every one of those days of the nine months in her womb, even though she longs to hold her baby in her arms. She watches every movement of the new-born baby, watching for signs of deafness, blindness, or some genetic defect that might show itself. She watches and waits over that baby for those precious early years, and it takes some time before she can relax, and be assured that all is well. She will give the baby all the time it needs to crawl, and to make gurgling sounds. These are foreshadowings of what is to come, and she cannot hurry up the process. All will come in God's own time.

Notice how many phrases we have about God and time. A young lad was speaking to God, and he asked him a question. 'What does a million years mean to you?' 'Oh, that's only like a second.' 'And what does a million pounds mean to you?' 'Oh, nothing more than a penny.' The boy pushed his luck a little farther. 'And would you give me a million pounds?' 'Of course I would', said God. 'When?' asked the boy. 'In a second' came the reply. 'A thousand years are but as yesterday; in a flash they are all gone.'

Our life-span must appear very very short in the eyes of God. I can imagine God wishing that we were not in such a great hurry to solve every problem today, and to make everything perfect yesterday. There's a time for everything under heaven. 'Slow down, you're going too fast. We've got to make the morning last ...' I meet people and I would love to reach into the small of their backs, find that winder, and unwind it a few notches! Nerves don't break own; people do. Life can get so taut as I reach with one hand to change yesterday, and with the other to arrange tomorrow ... and there's not much happening today.

Life is too precious not to savour the experience, and stop to smell the flowers. Sometimes I wait *on* others, but most times I have to wait *for* others. Punctuality can be a virtue, but it can turn a person into a tyrant, because some people will probably arrive late for their own funerals. This can be very frustrating, but it certainly is a wonderful opportunity for dying to self. I myself have wasted hundreds of hours in my life by being punctual. I am not good at waiting for others, especially as it's usually the same people all the time.

When I chose 'Waiting and Watching' as a title for this chapter, I was thinking of this solely in relation to God. I know now that I have wandered all over the place, even though I know that there is nothing in our lives that cannot be connected to God in some way or other. As I write this, God is waiting. He is waiting for me to turn to him. He is waiting for my 'yes', and for every opportunity to bless. Above all, he is waiting for that great moment when, like his Prodigal Son, I appear on the horizon. He wants me to be on my guard, to watch, because, as Peter says, 'Our adversary the devil goes about like a roaring lion seeking those he would devour.'

God wants us to be safe and secure in his world, and he wants us to know that he is constantly looking out for us. A young member of an Indian tribe was going through a rite of passage, to qualify as a warrior in the tribe. One of the tests involved him being placed in the midst of a jungle on his own for a night. As darkness fell, the whole place became eerie and creepie. His heart pounded with every sound in the undergrowth. He heard animals prowling and howling, and there wasn't the slightest hope that he was going to get any sleep that night. There were times he felt like running, but he knew it would be impossible to run anywhere in the jungle, in the dark of night. He never knew that a night could be so long. Finally, the dawn began to filter through the trees. It took some time before he could make out the shapes of the trees and the bushes. As his eyes became used to the growing light, he spotted something behind a tree nearby. He moved forward to investigate, and was amazed to find his father standing there with a gun. He was there all night, guarding over his son. The son's instant reaction was, 'If I had known that my father was looking over me like that, I would have slept soundly all night.'

That's what you'll discover when you die ... Don't wait till then to experience it ...

Right here right now

The only time that exists is now. Yesterday is gone, and will never return. I don't know what's coming next. It could be tomorrow, or it could be eternity; I don't know which will come first. 'Now is the time of salvation; today is the day of the Lord.'

The graces of today are very unique, and will never be repeated. Salvation is not something I get when I die. It is the grace I get to start again, any moment I choose to. All diets begin tomorrow! I am going to do great and good things, but it's always going to be 'at some other time'. When the house is finished, when the kids are reared, when I am retired. There is always going to be that 'ideal time' when things are going to happen, but *this* is not it! 'Some Sunday when there's no Mass' was a phrase used in my younger days. The grace of God is offered to us *now*, because, obviously, God sees that the grace is needed now.

It is a particular blessing to be a person of action, who is ready and willing to avail of the graces of God as they come along. In a novel by Albert Camus, called *The Fall*, there is a story about a man from the legal profession who is visiting Amsterdam. One night, he was in a red-light district, when he heard a woman scream. It sounded as if someone had thrown her into the canal. The man thought about what he should do. His first instinct was to go to her assistance. The more he thought about it, the less attractive than option became. What if the police came along? What if the press arrived, and his picture appeared in the paper in this particular part of town. Maybe the person who attacked her was still around, and would attack him as well. Very soon the screaming stopped and, by now, the man knew it would be too late to do anything anyhow. Camus completes the story with a chilling and damning comment. He didn't do anything, because that's the kind of man he was.

'Life is what happens when you're making other plans' are

words attributed to John Lennon. There is another powerful phrase, and I'm not sure who first spoke it, but it is 'There is nothing more powerful than an idea whose time has come.' There is no scarcity of ideas. We all have many bright and brilliant ideas; but how many of them will be put into operation? 'The road to hell is paved with good intentions'. We will all die with a long list of things that 'we never got around to'!

To understand the Spirit is to understand, and to act on his inspirations. If an idea is a good one, it should be acted on. Of course, we cannot do everything, and there will be many things left undone. What I'm speaking about here is acting promptly when the inspiration comes, if time and circumstances allow. Procrastination is the thief of time. Acting on inspiration is often nothing more than obeying God's commands. It is really a question of obedience.

Jesus speaks about the man with the two sons. He asked one son to do something, and he said he would, but he didn't. He asked the other son to do something, and he said he wouldn't, but he did. Jesus makes it clear that it is what each lad did that matters, and not what each one said. One of the ways in which we'll never get around to doing anything is to think about it long enough, to quote from *Peter Calvey Hermit*. How often do we debate a problem, set up a committee to 'look into it', issue a report for our consideration, and the problem is still untouched and unsolved?

The hungry people of the world may have to wait for many more G8 Summits before the world's surplus food is made available to them. There is no scarcity of food. Half the world is dying of hunger, and the other half is on a diet, trying to get down the weight. What is lacking is the will to do something about it, by those who are in a position to do so.

I remember hearing something a few years ago that went somewhat like this: You say that if you came across a group of people who are radically living the gospel, you would join them. I tell you that that is not the case. When you are *ready* to radically live the gospel, you will find that group. Otherwise, there could be one such group on your doorstep, and you have never noticed them, and you will never notice them. When you are ready to radically live the gospel, you will find that group very quickly. In fact, if you are ready and willing to radically live the gospel, you will begin such a group, if there isn't one there already. It's those people of action who get things done around here.

I remember some years ago, speaking to one of our priests who was working with lepers in Calcutta. His stories were gripping and many of them were horrendous. I said to him, 'What do you think someone like me could do to help such a situation?' His answer was immediate and spontaneous. 'Stay at home, and start at home.' When I was growing up we always had a prayer among our Rosary 'trimmings' 'for the conversion of Russia'. That was safe enough, because it had to do with other people being converted. It helped make us more smug than we were! We collected pennies for 'black babies in Africa'. The further away the problem the better, and the safer we felt.

When someone speaks to us about our conversion, it can become a little uncomfortable. 'We shall all one day die' is safe enough; but to say that 'I shall one day die' gets too close for comfort. Stay at home, and start at home. When it comes to concern for the welfare of others, I can begin right here, right now, with the person nearest to me. I may be concerned about people in Iraq, and not speaking to a neighbour across the street.

I have listed many insights in this book so far, but I think I can honestly say that it was only when I acted on them that they led me to anything good. Insights can be wonderful if you write books or give Retreats. For some years now I have got into a certain attitude when I'm writing a book. I write for me. I write so that I myself can reflect and mull over my thoughts, and discover what benefit they have brought to my life. The fact that somebody else is going to read these when the book comes out does not concern me in the least. I do not write for others, because I can see the danger inherent in that. I can only write with any conviction about these insights if they have played a role in my own growth, and I can identify the good that flowed from them.

'Bloom where you're planted' is wise advice. Some years ago I was speaking to a Sister in an active congregation of nuns who was considering entering an enclosed community of Sisters. The idea was admirable, and she was a good person. As I questioned her, I was looking for the answer to one question. Was she entering an enclosed congregation so that she might become holy? If so, then she should stay where she is. Any one of us can become holy exactly where we are. We all are surrounded by the very people who will make us holy. If she was entering because she had a vocation to the Contemplative Life, fair enough; she should go ahead.

We have saints from any and every walk of life, like St Joseph Labouré who spent his life sleeping rough on the streets of Rome. St Leopold was a Capuchin monk in Padua not so very long ago. He had a stammer, so he couldn't preach. This led him to spend his time in the Confessional. His ministry there became so powerful that people came from all over the world to go to Confession to him. He was canonised a few years ago. Another Capuchin, Fr Solanus Casey, is on the fast-track for canonisation. He never could pass his moral theology exams, so he was never allowed hear Confessions. He spent his life at the front desk in reception in the friary. He signed Mass cards, and listened to people's problems. Once again, word got out about him, and the friary became a focal point for people far and near, seeking prayers and blessings.

If I went to live in a cave in the Dublin mountains, and I give myself completely to the Lord and to his will, there will be a pathway up the side of the mountain in no time at all, as people will seek me out, looking for a share in the blessings the Lord is pouring out upon me. The more Thomas Merton tried to withdraw into his hermitage, the more people came to him, many from very far away. The person of God attracts people like a lamp draws the moth.

I said earlier that everyone of us has within our lives whatever it takes to make us holy. To be able to look around me at the people, situations, and circumstances of my life, and to say 'yes' is to bloom where I'm planted. The safest place in the whole world for me to be is where God wants me to be. The most important place for me in the whole world is right here at this desk; and the most important time in my whole life is this very moment that is passing. God is to be found in the ordinary.

St Zita is the patron saint of pots and pans! Most people that I know are doing an excellent job exactly where they are. Parents continue to impress me by their generosity of spirit. A friend, who is a mother, told me that being a parent is very demanding, but the rewards are truly wonderful.

None of us can measure our own holiness, nor should we dare try to do so! Holiness is what happens to me, like a baby getting teeth or hair. There is nothing the baby can do to hurry up the process. Each day brings its own growth, and only the most observant of mothers will notice this happening.

In the very first chapter of this book, I spoke about God being able to see the very best in all of us. He sees the part of us that reflects his image. He has planted us *here*, and he has given us *now*, and with that comes all that we need to grow, and become what God created us to be. We are truly blessed right here, right now. But the best is yet to come. You ain't seen nothing yet …